A PLUME BOOK

THIS LAND IS OUR LAND

Cadence Cook

KEN ILGUNAS is an author, journalist, and backcountry ranger in Alaska. He has hitchhiked ten thousand miles across North America, paddled one thousand miles across Ontario in a birchbark canoe, and walked 1,700 miles across the Great Plains, following the proposed route of the Keystone XL pipeline. Ilgunas has a BA from SUNY Buffalo in history and English, and an MA in liberal studies from Duke University. The author of travel memoirs *Walden on Wheels* and *Trespassing Across America*, he is from Wheatfield, New York.

ALSO BY KEN ILGUNAS

Walden on Wheels

Trespassing Across America

THIS LAND IS
OUR LAND

HOW WE LOST THE
RIGHT TO ROAM AND
HOW TO TAKE IT BACK

KEN ILGUNAS

PLUME

PLUME
An imprint of Penguin Random House LLC
375 Hudson Street
New York, New York 10014

Copyright © 2018 by Ken Ilgunas
Penguin supports copyright. Copyright fuels creativity, encourages diverse voices, promotes free speech, and creates a vibrant culture. Thank you for buying an authorized edition of this book and for complying with copyright laws by not reproducing, scanning, or distributing any part of it in any form without permission. You are supporting writers and allowing Penguin to continue to publish books for every reader.

THIS LAND IS YOUR LAND
Words and Music by Woody Guthrie
WGP/TRO-© Copyright 1956, 1958, 1970, 1972, and 1995 (copyrights renewed) Woody Guthrie Publications, Inc. & Ludlow Music, Inc., New York, NY, administered by Ludlow Music, Inc.
Used by Permission.

Plume is a registered trademark and its colophon is a trademark of Penguin Random House LLC.

Library of Congress Cataloging-in-Publication Data
has been applied for.

ISBN 9780735217843 (paperback)
ISBN 9780735217850 (eBook)

Printed in the United States of America
1   3   5   7   9   10   8   6   4   2

Book design by Eve Kirch

For my best friends, Josh and David

*Was a high wall there that tried to stop me
A sign was painted said: Private Property,
But on the back side it didn't say nothing—
This land was made for you and me.*

—Original verse from "This Land Is
Your Land" by Woody Guthrie

Contents

CONTENTS

Introduction

It is not in the nature of human beings to be cattle in glorified feedlots. Every person deserves the option to travel easily in and out of the complex and primal world that gave us birth. We need freedom to roam across land owned by no one but protected by all, whose unchanging horizon is the same that bounded the world of our millennial ancestors.

—E. O. Wilson, *The Creation*[1]

In his poem "Mending Wall," New England poet Robert Frost and his neighbor repair a stone wall that separates their properties. It's their annual tradition. Each spring, they rough up their hands lifting and setting the fallen stones, playfully casting spells on the wobbling wall to "Stay where you are until our backs are turned!"

There's irony in repairing an unneighborly wall because the two neighbors are indeed neighborly as they work across from one another. To Frost, the wall makes no sense because it only divides him from his good neighbor, as well as Frost's harmless apple trees from his neighbor's harmless pines. "Something there is that doesn't love a wall," Frost muses. The neighbor, as well, isn't quite sure why they have the wall. When Frost asks him why they rebuild it every year, the neighbor can only recite the saying of his father: "Good fences make good neighbours." Even Frost, with his doubts and musings, feels strangely compelled to take part in—even initiate—the yearly tradition.

The way I read it, Frost's poem isn't just about walls, divisions, or neighbors. At its core, the poem grapples with the trouble of unquestioned tradition and the gravitational pull of precedent. "Mending Wall" urges us to rethink our traditions, specifically our tradition of closing off lands to our fellow countrymen and women. So let's think about the poem, not from the perspective of two neighbors in the year 1914 in New England, but from the perspective of 324 million people in twenty-first-century America, a country arguably more divided now than it's been since the Civil War. Let's think about our own unquestioned devotion to fences, to "No Trespassing" signs, and to an unbending understanding of private property. Let's think about why we, as a matter of course, forbid our fellow citizens from our lands.

This book calls for the right to roam across America. It calls for opening up private land for public hiking, camping, and other harmless forms of recreation. Skeptics, and more than a few landowners, may reasonably argue that bringing into question something as sacrosanct and entrenched in American culture as private property would be, in our present world, a rather ridiculous notion. Considering how there are no ongoing movements calling for the right to roam, no proposed bills, and no politicians lobbying to open up private land, one might argue that what I'm proposing is fantastical, unreasonable, and just plain foolhardy, especially when our country is plagued by problems more serious than our nature deficit disorders and recreational access issues. One could charge that I'm tilting at windmills, that I'm advocating for something unattainable, that I'm calling for changing an institution that many Americans in fact cherish.

To these charges, I'd have to answer, "Maybe so." But I would also argue that our problems with physical and mental health, of dwindling green spaces, of environmental injustice, and of inequality in land ownership are all serious and will only get worse in the decades to come. If things keep going the way they are, then by the end of the twenty-first century few of us will have access to our last havens of natural space and to the vanishing pleasures of solitude, peace, adventure, and the hundred other benefits that spring from a relationship with the natural world. That's hardly a bold prediction, because today, early in the first half of the twenty-first century, few of us have easy access to these places and the feelings they stir.

Should you be turned off by what may be a radical, or even heretical, idea, let's remind ourselves that there is no harm in thinking for the future, even the deep future. If it makes it easier to read, then consider this book a book for the twenty-second century—a book that calls for something unlikely right now but plants a seed that may one day grow branches under which future generations may walk. (Beware: Many more hiking metaphors to come.) At the very least, I hope this book encourages us to think about an institution that is so ever present that we seldom give it a thought and that we accept without scruple. I speak of property, specifically our American brand of absolute and exclusionary private property.

Now that I've performed the delicate footwork of (hopefully) assuring the reader that this book has not in fact been written with a thoughtless zeal, a reckless radicalness (or a certifiable insanity), I hope you'll join me as I take a bold step forward, through the gaps in our fallen walls and unmended fences, into the great American countryside, where I believe we'd be a better nation if we did away with the faulty notion that "good fences make good neighbours." I believe the opposite to be true.

Ken Ilgunas, 2017

THIS LAND IS
OUR LAND

CHAPTER 1

The Right to Roam

My first years were spent living just as my fore-fathers had lived—roaming the green, rolling hills.[2]

—Chief Luther Standing Bear,
Land of the Spotted Eagle, 1933

As a travel writer, I have the bad habit of writing about myself. I plant forests of *I's* over pages and leave behind trails of thoughts and feelings that I think will change the world but that only succeed in embarrassing me. A historical and political book of this nature warrants a more formal and less personal style. While this book, outside of this chapter, may come across as impersonal, I do wish to say up front that it has in fact been written with passion and feeling. For me, the seemingly boring subjects of property law, land-use planning, and public-access legislation are, well, personal.

Let me start by telling you about where I grew up. On the western edge of New York State, between the cities of Buffalo and Niagara Falls, is Wheatfield. Sprawling over twenty-eight square miles of mostly flat land and bordered on one end by the mighty

Niagara River, Wheatfield was not too long ago a countryside of forests and cornfields.

Before white settlers moved into the area in the mid-1800s, the land was a relatively untouched forest inhabited by Native American tribes. Wheatfield's soil is well suited for growing wheat, so when the settlers arrived, wheat became a local staple. Then came the Erie Canal. Then industry grew, both in Buffalo and Niagara Falls. And in the second half of the twentieth century, the middle class fled the cities to live out the suburban American Dream. In less than two hundred years, the character of the land shifted from wild to farm to suburb.

If you drive through Wheatfield today, you might not be all that impressed. The town's schools, churches, pizzerias, ballparks, retirement homes, and shopping centers are scattered incoherently. You'd see that it's just yet another poorly planned American town, aggressively developed without aesthetic vision or forethought. Its natural beauties—of which there are plenty—are obscured by the fast roads, endless subdivisions, and RV dealership monstrosities. It is, shall we say, a town without charm. Since there is no Main Street, town center, or civic landmark, it's a stretch to even call it a "town," with all the connotations of cohesion that being a town implies.

Yet it is a place that remains happy and peaceful in my dreams, for it was—for a time at least—a boyhood paradise. My family was among the first to move into a subdivision in Wheatfield called Country Meadows. During our first couple of years in Country Meadows, my brother and I would play in a thin stand of woods between our backyard and a cornfield. In the adjoining lot, still wild and vacant, we skated on a pond in the winter and collected tadpoles from it in the summer.

A bunch of new families had just moved to Wheatfield, which back in the late 1980s was mostly farms and fields. We were all strangers. We were all trespassers. There weren't any grouchy old landowners. There weren't any exclusionary signs, rules, or customs. It was a suburb without fences. It was a countryside without guns. And it was suddenly populated by a bunch of excited working-class families who'd just bought their first homes.

My boyhood friends and I roamed over the muddied construction lots, passed through woods, and extended our little football fields and baseball diamonds onto our neighbors' newly planted lawns. We played in the neighborhood's half-constructed homes, some of us laying siege to our friends inside those plywood castles with an artillery of mud clumps. We stole scrap lumber and built forts in the woods behind my home. My family let our golden retriever out, night or day, to sniff and chase and wander where he wished, unleashed. Later, as teenagers, we walked between homes to play football on a huge stretch of grass behind our subdivision. We never thought to ask who owned that grass.

I remember the storms of cawing blackbirds that would descend to feed on our back lawn. I remember the stink of the freshly manured cornfield. I remember the humid summer nights, the smell of raw pumpkin pulp, the lawns bronzed with blankets of fall foliage. I remember the snow tunnels and snowball wars. In all of my years in Country Meadows, I can remember only one sharp word from a homeowner for trespassing. For the most part, I remember a land without fences. Without signs. Without prohibitions.

But don't let me paint too idyllic a picture. My adolescence wasn't all skinned knees and wilderness adventures. And I was no Huck Finn. I spent plenty of time inside, too, playing more than my share of video games and watching more than my share of TV. These were the 1990s, after all. There were Saturday morning cartoons, Sega games, air-conditioning, and many other things that tempted us to remain indoors. But it was also a time before the Internet, before the ubiquity of home computers, before helicopter parents, and before kids owned their own phones. My friends and I, more often than not, left the comforts of home to roam the neighborhood unsupervised to play until dark.

Our rural-suburban dream wouldn't last forever, though. As my brother and I grew up, Wheatfield's rural landscape was swiftly changing character. Nearby fields became smothered in asphalt. Forests were hacked down to make way for yet more subdivisions. Between 1990 and 2010, over three thousand housing units were added, and the town's population increased 39 percent, from eleven thousand to eighteen thousand people.[3] It was one of the fastest-growing towns in all of New York State.

My neighborhood expanded like the rest of Wheatfield, and this is just a small sample of what has been happening in America since World War II. According to the United States Department of Agriculture, between 1982 and 2007 forty-one million acres of American forest and farmland were bulldozed,[4] largely because of urban growth, reducing our country's forest and farmland by about the size of Wisconsin.

These days in Country Meadows there are no green spaces for kids to explore anymore. There's no more collecting tadpoles. There are no more woods for building forts, no more ponds for ice-skating. Walk the roads and you'll see new "No Trespassing" signs around the remaining woods. The dogs are all safely locked behind electric fences. There are no sidewalks or public trails. The subdivision itself is quiet, gets little traffic, and is good for a stroll. But walkers and cyclists are essentially locked inside a couple of adjacent subdivisions by a surrounding network of noisy and dangerous roads. If you happen to see someone walking or cycling outside of the development on one of these busy streets, you assume that they're either destitute or crazy.

I begin this book in Wheatfield not because the place is unusual. I begin it in Wheatfield because Wheatfield is so ordinary. Many Americans, whether in cities, suburbs, or even rural areas, lack green places and safe places to walk. Most of our cities and towns have been developed with drivers in mind, not pedestrians. Every year, vehicles kill thousands of Americans out walking. The organization Smart Growth America reported that from 2003 to 2012 more than 47,000 pedestrians were killed (sixteen times the number of Americans killed by tornadoes, hurricanes, floods, and earthquakes combined), and an estimated 676,000 were injured walking along roads.[5]

Our lack of safe and peaceful walking places may contribute to our status as one of the more sedentary countries in the world. In 2010, the journal *Medicine & Science in Sports & Exercise* reported that Americans walked an average of 5,117 steps a day, almost half of what the health community recommends[6]

and far fewer than the averages of the other countries the researchers studied, including Australia
(9,695), Switzerland (9,650), and Japan (7,168).[7]
According to a 2012 study by *The Lancet*, 41 percent
of Americans qualify as sedentary for not getting
the recommended 150 minutes of exercise per
week.[8] In 2015, the National Center for Health Statistics reported that, among Americans over twenty
years old, 71 percent are overweight and 38 percent
are obese.[9]

Today, from my family's front door, there is essentially no practical or scenic place to walk to—no
store, no community center, no church, no forest
grove, no flowery meadow—so the only walkers are
the recreation walkers, and we are far too few. Many
of my friends, family, and neighbors have suffered
as a result. People I love and care about have weight
problems and diseases like type 2 diabetes. The
people of my neighborhood are generally civically
disengaged and socially isolated. In Country Meadows, I remember one block party from my youth,
when one especially sociable family hosted a giant
get-together on their lawn, with drinks for the adults
and games for the kids. But that was an exception
to the rule. Most neighbors don't talk or even wave
hello when passing each other by. My family has lived
in this neighborhood since 1989, yet we don't know
the names of our neighbors just two houses down.

Don't get me wrong: Country Meadows is a *good*
neighborhood. In Country Meadows, there is no
crime or gang violence. You don't have to lock your
doors when you leave the house. Kids don't even
smash pumpkins anymore. But just because it's free
of hardship and suffering doesn't mean that we can't

call for something better—a Country Meadows, perhaps, where everyone has more access to nature, a greater sense of freedom, and better health.

Since graduating from college, I've called a number of other places home. I moved to the rolling red-clay hills of the North Carolina Piedmont, where on the roads around me I estimate that three out of every five property owners have posted "No Trespassing" signs. Barred from these woodlands, walkers are forced to stay on winding, shoulderless roads. We walkers have to keep an eye out for reckless drivers, and we can anticipate a belligerent honk or two. In York County, Nebraska, I lived in between corn and soybean fields, where virtually every foot of green space was devoted to industrial agriculture.

One solution to our walking problems is to design better communities with safe walking in mind. Our country's leading walking organization, America Walks, is working toward this goal. And books like Jeff Speck's *Walkable City* and *Suburban Nation* discuss how we can design our cities and suburbs better. A pleasant walk to the post office, though, only gets you so far.

A more radical solution—which is the subject of this book—is "the right to roam." The right to roam is an American tradition dating back to our nation's origins, when ordinary folks had the right to walk through privately owned woods and fields, and along the coasts. While this may seem like a vestige of our past, gone forever like the flocks of passenger pigeons whose migrations once darkened our skies, there is reason for hope. In several European countries this freedom has been reborn and is thriving, suggesting that it can be reborn here.

I've fallen in love with the right to roam. Maybe it started when I was a boy, when I got to roam my half-built suburb as I wished. Or maybe it was later in life when I took offense at all the "No Trespassing" signs. Or maybe it was in northern Alaska, where I lived and worked and could walk wherever I wanted. With a map in one hand and a compass in the other, I walked up and over mountain passes of the Brooks Range and along the cobbled banks of the Koyukuk River, where hikers keep an eye out for moose and grizzlies lurking in the spruce forests. I drank freely from streams and rivers, I collected wild blueberries and cranberries, and I got to experience the exhilarating sense of solitude—and the bolstered sense of self-reliance—that comes from a walk alone through wilderness.

After the complete freedom of Alaska, it wasn't easy coming back to an off-limits landscape. America, to me, suddenly felt like it had too many fences, signs, and rules. So I spent my twenties seeking out our world's remaining roamable places. For a summer, I canoed across the waterways of Ontario, Canada. I hiked over the Scottish Highlands and down historic English paths. I would go back to Alaska each summer to work as a backcountry park ranger, roaming over the valleys and mountains of the roadless and pathless Gates of the Arctic National Park.

Most notably, in 2012, I embarked on a hiking journey over the proposed route of the Keystone XL pipeline, which was planned to stretch 1,700 miles over the Great Plains, from Alberta in Canada to the Gulf Coast of Texas. To walk over the pipeline's route, roads wouldn't do. Rather, I'd have to cross fields, hop barbed-wire fences, and camp in cow pastures—all on private property. To go on this hike, I'd essentially have to trespass across America. I hiked over Montana grasslands, through South Dakota canyons, and across Nebraska cornfields. I watched Kansas sunsets, Oklahoma sunrises, and camped on the soft beds of Texas pine needles. Most days, I felt as though I had the whole Great Plains to myself. I walked over rolling wide-open grasslands beneath an enormous prairie sky, where cloud-mountains sailed off into distant horizons. Every day, I'd watch herds of deer or white-bellied, dark-nosed pronghorn soar across the prairie like comets, leaving behind trails of shuddering grass. In a hay-field in Saskatchewan, I watched thousands of ducks rise and circle the field like the slow rotation of clouds before a twister touches down. It was a countryside so peaceful and so pretty that I often felt as though I was in the deep backcountry of a national park.

These places, though, are off-limits to Americans. The places I illegally hiked over and the sights I enjoyed are for the exclusive pleasure of a few farmers and ranchers. If you travel across rural America, you'll see "No Trespassing" and "Private Property" signs on trees and fence posts everywhere. And even where there are no signs, Americans know that they don't have implicit permission to visit the woods or fields surrounding their town. Long gone are the days when Americans could freely wander "through the woods and over the hills and fields, absolutely free from all worldly engagements," as Henry David Thoreau did in the countryside around his hometown of Concord, Massachusetts.[10]

On your next drive through the countryside, count how many people you see, whether they're working, playing, or just lounging. Look over the fields, into the forests, down the rows in vineyards and apple orchards. Perhaps you'll spot a few workers during picking time, or maybe a farmer harvesting his crops in his combine. But, for the most part, you'll see nobody. These are our unvisited countrysides. These were once theaters of activity where Americans worked and played, but now they're closed off to us by gates, barbed wire, and laws.

Consider how many of these places are off-limits to Americans. According to the USDA's ownership survey in 1999, only 3.4 million of us[11] (or 1.2 percent of the population) owned agricultural land, which makes up 49 percent of the land in the Lower Forty-Eight states. It looks even worse when you factor in the low levels of ethnic minority land ownership. Ethnic minorities make up 38 percent of the US population, but, according to the USDA's 2014 Tenure, Ownership, and Transition of Agricultural Land Survey, 97 percent of agricultural landlords are white.[12] This means an overwhelmingly white 1 percent of the population has the right to exclude 99 percent of Americans from 49 percent of the land in the Lower Forty-Eight states.

Let's put aside agricultural land for a second and look at just how unequally private land is shared in the United States. The most recent data that looked at the distribution of land ownership among income groups was in 1978. (Land ownership data is difficult to collect and there is no national database, hence the absence of up-to-date data.) In 1978, the data showed that the wealthiest Americans, or the top 1 percent, owned 48 percent of the private land by acreage. The top 5 percent owned 75 percent of private land.[13] These statistics are old, but it may be safe to infer that land ownership inequality, since then, has stayed the same or has gotten worse alongside wealth inequality. These past forty or so years, the United States has seen its wealth inequality spiral out of control, reaching levels not experienced since 1928, the eve of the Great Depression.[14] According to the Economic Policy Institute, in 1978 CEOs made thirty times more than their workers. In 2015, CEOs made 275 times more. During that period, CEOs saw a 941 percent increase in compensation, versus 10 percent for workers.[15] Now the wealthiest .1 percent own 22 percent of the wealth in the United States, as much wealth as the bottom 90 percent.[16] With these numbers in mind, it's probably fair to assume that land distribution hasn't gotten any more equal. Some of today's landowners own giant properties that would be the envy of medieval lords and monarchs. According to *The Land Report,* the top one hundred landowners in America own close to 38 million acres, which is 1.5 percent of all American land or 2.3 percent of all American private land.[17] Ted Turner and John Malone, cable television and media billionaires, together own 4.2 million acres, amounting to 2.5 times the size of Delaware.

Or consider corporate ownership of American land. The top ten private industrial timber companies own 23 million acres of American land. (America's biggest timber giant, Weyerhaeuser, after its 2016 merger with Plum Creek, owns 13 million acres.) There are 766 million acres of forest in the

United States, and about 19 percent of this land, or 147 million acres, is corporate-owned industrial forestland.[18] In other words, the corporate timber industry owns a staggering 6 percent of America. The coal industry, according to a report by the Appalachian Land Ownership Task Force, owns 20 million acres just in Appalachia. In the area studied in Virginia, West Virginia, Kentucky, Tennessee, North Carolina, and Alabama in the late 1970s, researchers found that 1 percent of the population owned 53 percent of the land.[19] As for farmland, the USDA estimates that almost a third of all farmland is owned by "non-operator landlords." Corporations, trusts, and other owners own an estimated 10 percent of farmland, or 91 million acres.[20] Madeleine Fairbairn, a professor at UC Santa Cruz, said financial service companies, starting around 2008, started to take an interest in purchasing farmland because farmland is stable income for the likes of hedge funds, college endowments, and pension funds. TIAA, a retirement provider, began investing heavily in farmland in 2007 and now controls $8 billion of farmland globally. "We're in the beginning stages of what could be a significant shift in land ownership," Fairbairn has said.

Much of our country's private lands have fallen into just a few hands, and there's also an emerging crisis with the management and ownership of our public lands.

Consider the trends, which I'll discuss in more detail in Chapter 6.

1. Our national parks are overrun with people. In 2016, there were a record 331 million visits to our national parks, up from a record 307 million visits the year before.[21] Many parks have been so flooded with visitors that, despite coming to "get away," visitors often end up in traffic that's as bad as in many cities.

2. Despite a demand for public recreation spaces, we're actually _losing_ federal lands. The four agencies that manage public recreation lands—the Forest Service, National Park Service, Fish and Wildlife Service, and Bureau of Land Management—have lost more than 17 million acres of federal land since 1990.*[22]

3. Demand for public recreation spaces will only increase as the population grows. US census projections show that we can expect our population to grow by almost another 100 million people—to 417 million—by 2060.[23] The more people we have, the more congested our parks will become.

4. We're losing our _private_ green spaces, too. A 2012 report by the US Forest Service predicted that urban and developed areas in the United States will increase by between 41 and 77 percent by 2060,[24] which means that as many as 69 million additional acres of farm, range, and forestland (about the size of Colorado) could be developed within the next forty years.

Imagine how well our already overrun national parks will be able to serve our country's recreation

---

* Most of these federal lands have been lost in Alaska, where the land has been transferred to Alaskan tribes exercising their right to claim federal land.

needs when the country has less green space and another hundred million people.

―――――

While I was writing my travel book *Trespassing Across America*, I was fascinated to learn from my research that people in other countries can do legally what I did illegally. In Sweden, they call it *allemansrätten*. In Finland, it's *jokamiehenoikeus*. In Great Britain, it's simply the "right to roam." These are the terms that describe an ordinary citizen's right to roam on open land, whether that land is publicly or privately owned. In these countries, citizens can travel, camp, enjoy nature, and feel like free people.

If we opened up the portion of our country that is privately owned we would have an additional billion and a half acres for countryside recreation: 614 million acres of grassland pasture, 408 million acres of cropland, approximately 444 million acres of privately owned forest, and thousands of miles of river, lake, and ocean shorelines.[25] We could finally walk along the Loess Hills of Iowa, a range of bluffs and crests that run down the state alongside the Missouri River. Or we could imagine walking with bare feet up and down New England's coast. Or we could freely stroll down the cornstalk corridors of Nebraska's section lines, snowshoe over the harvested winter fields of Wisconsin, hike the rolling farm valleys of Ohio, or camp beneath the dark starlit skies of the Texas plains. There would be new recreational opportunities in every state.

To be clear, opening up private property does not mean the end of private property. Landowners in right-to-roam countries still own their land.

Landowners are allowed to use the land as they wish and can halt interferences with their own activities. Landowners are allowed their due privacy. In other words, one can fully support both private property *and* the right to roam over private property.

Opening up these pastures, croplands, forests, and shorelines would provide recreational space for nearly everybody. Access to these places would also make us feel something that we Americans greatly value but seldom get to experience in a profound way: freedom.

We may not realize it, but there is, deep in the American subconscious, a love for roaming. To be able to roam is the mark of a free and adventurous life. To roam is not merely to walk. To roam is to explore. To roam is to blaze our own trail and find our own way. Roaming is an act of nonconformity, of independence, of self-reliance. Our culture romanticizes braving the elements and overcoming the challenges of a wild countryside. In practice we may be automobile drivers, but in spirit we are roamers.

Roaming is in our folklore and our cultural DNA. Our most celebrated folk heroes, real and fictional— Johnny Appleseed, Daniel Boone, Davy Crockett, Buffalo Bill, Calamity Jane, Sacagawea, Paul Bunyan, the Lone Ranger—have been idolized because they got to roam over early America. (Just about every parent in the United States speaks approvingly of a large man who rides his sleigh and reindeer over our yards and trespasses down our chimneys each Christmas.) We glorify the roaming culture of Native Americans, and even celebrate Red Cloud, Sitting Bull, and Geronimo—defiant figures who valiantly fought US forces to safeguard native people's way of life. In the Black Hills of South Dakota, we are currently sculpting what may become the biggest statue in the world—a memorial (many times bigger than Mount Rushmore) to Crazy Horse, the iconic Lakota warrior who is remembered to have said, "One does not sell the earth upon which the people walk."[26]

Our literature is full of characters who roam, from Mark Twain's Huck Finn to James Fenimore Cooper's Leatherstocking. Popular books of the last century urge that we heed *The Call of the Wild*, that we venture *Into the Wild*, or that we simply be *Wild*. The joy of going wherever we please is everywhere in our popular culture. The Hunger Games' Katniss Everdeen had her woods for hunting, and the child heroes in classic eighties adventure movies—*E.T.*, *The Goonies*, *Stand by Me*, or the recent hot new series *Stranger Things*—all had woods and caverns to freely explore. "No Trespassing" signs do not hold these characters back. America's favorite shows and books and movies—The Lord of the Rings, Harry Potter, Star Wars, *Avatar*, and *Game of Thrones*—contain characters who roam their worlds, and every Western ever written or filmed featured cowboys and Indians wandering where they liked. Kids today watch heroes in *Toy Story*, *Up*, *Finding Nemo*, *Brave*, *Moana*, and *The Jungle Book* have grand, uninhibited adventures in urban, suburban, and wild landscapes. We are drawn to "man vs. nature" TV shows like *Man vs. Wild*, *Survivorman*, and *Naked and Afraid*. We grow up playing video games—*Super Mario*, *The Legend of Zelda*, *Skyrim*, *Assassin's Creed*, *World of Warcraft*—in which we have our digital avatars roam through virtual 3-D wildernesses, which are sometimes enormous in size. (The computer game *Guild Wars Nightfall* is set in a world that contains fifteen thousand square miles of explorable terrain.)[27]

Roaming is represented as the ultimate way to live a life of freedom, but we are forbidden from living that life. We've normalized and internalized our status as "trespassers." We *know* that the field we drive past on our commute to work each day is off-limits. We *know* that we are confined to public beaches. We *know* that to go on a walk we must stick to roads. We've all been driving by, walking past, and looking at our off-limits countryside from afar for more than a hundred years, seldom thinking that it ought to be our right to have access to all that land. We grow so used to seeing but never experiencing the places around us that they become little more than an oilcloth backdrop rather than the living, breathing three-dimensional world they are. Tell someone that you're going to walk over that private field and there's a good chance that they'll smile and warn you that you'll "get shot." The image of the American landowner as a fiery, gun-wielding, property-guarding Yosemite Sam and our deep-seated understanding of private property as off-limits no-man's-lands restrain us from placing our feet on land that, under a different set of laws and with a different frame of mind, could be as much ours as his. So entrenched is our sense of ourselves as trespassers that we cannot conceive of rights that are unalienable to many Europeans. We fail to see how one of the most joyful and essential of human liberties—freely enjoying a walk in nature—has been stolen from under our noses.

Despite these stolen liberties, we still talk about being a free country. But how many people in America *feel* free? Most of us are weighed down with back-breaking debts. We are compelled to give some corporation forty hours of our week. Our "liberating" wilderness excursions are limited to a weekend hunting trip or an annual visit to a national park, where we sit in congested traffic for hours and, at best, go for a hike on a trail along with a noisy parade of people. America is "the land of the free and the home of the brave," yet wherever we go we see an America that is fenced off and posted with "No Trespassing" signs. We have become the land of the sedentary and the home of the scared.

In historian Frederick Jackson Turner's 1893 essay "The Significance of the Frontier in American History" (in which he advanced his "frontier thesis" argument), Turner claimed that the American frontier was the most influential force in the making of the American character. Early Americans' proximity to "the meeting point between savagery and civilization" made Americans into hardy, freedom-loving, self-reliant citizens. Today, Americans still uphold these traits as uniquely American values, yet how many of us are actually this way? How many of us get to routinely experience wild land or live adventurous lives?

For the first century of America's existence, our right to roam and our relationship with wild land distinguished us from marginalized Europeans. So it's an irony of history that Europeans have regained access to nature while we Americans are corralled in suburban cul-de-sacs from which there is no escape. The truth is, our American folk heroes and our favorite movie characters would find that present-day America is quite dull. Here, Frodo Baggins, Daniel Boone, and Katniss Everdeen would either be fined for trespassing or would have to drive for hours—days even—to hold their adventures on legally traversable public lands.

———

In my neighborhood of Country Meadows, in the span of just a couple of decades, what was once a great freedom for one generation of kids no longer exists for the next. Today, the kids of Country Meadows don't mourn the loss of their green spaces and the chance to roam that my brother and I had—not because they don't care for these places or those rights but because they can't mourn something that they never knew. Our right to roam has gone the way of our starry skies, our clean air, our stable climate, and our hundred other stolen inheritances. Our civilization has been built atop the unmarked graves of these lost rights and forgotten joys. While we unknowingly walk over them—so close but so hidden from view—we accept as normal the creeping anxieties, the depressions, the sinking feelings of incompleteness that hang over our modern lives. We blame ourselves, we call ourselves weak, we medicate, and we never think to place some of the blame on the theft of our long-gone but unmourned rights.

I could forget about my boyhood in Country Meadows. Or that time I first felt complete freedom as a young man in Alaska. Or the simple joy of walking across my country. Honestly, now that I've had my share of wild nature, I could probably get by just fine with a treadmill, a yearly trip to a crowded national park, and a housebound life. You can probably get by, too. But I think we should aspire to something more than just "getting by." I think we should strive, if just for the sake of future generations, to reclaim our most fundamental human rights. I want to remember the hockey pond that my brother and I skated on. I want to remember the first time I saw a herd of caribou in the Brooks Range. I want to remember the never-before-felt wild joy that I carried in my chest for hours over the Great Plains beneath a wide blue South Dakota sky. I want to remember the right to roam with the hope that everyone someday might have access to something like these memories, these places, and the feelings they stir.

Let's remember our old fields and forests. Let's remember our old freedoms. Let's remember the land the way it once was. Let's remember the green spaces, the common lands, the adventurous lives that kids once got to lead. And if you didn't have these places, these rights, or these experiences, let's remember them anyway. Because, whether or not you had them as a child, they're in our country's history, our cultural DNA, our hunter-gatherer bodies. We must remember. Because not until a lost right is remembered, mourned, and felt can it be reclaimed.

On my hike across the Great Plains, I came to believe that property owners should not have the right to exclude others from land that no person, no country, and no god can truly own. We all should have a right to these green spaces. And a country should strive to give every one of its citizens the opportunity to walk safely, to explore freely, and to roam boldly.

Might reopening the countryside help us recapture some of the pioneer spirit that helped our country thrive? Might the right to roam give Americans the room to stretch their legs and embark on life-changing adventures? Might our lives be richer if we could walk our dogs in nearby fields, or camp in neighboring woods? I came to believe that something as innocent and wholesome as a walk across my country shouldn't be illegal. It should be every person's right.

CHAPTER 2

The Closing of America

Jehovah gave us verdant hills and sighing woods and babbling rills, and ponds as clear as glass; but man has fenced things in, we see, and nailed to every post and tree his sign, "Keep Off the Grass."

—Walt Mason, "Keep Off," 1919[28]

Before we reopen America's land, we might like to stop closing it down. Take, for instance, the unusual and somewhat ghoulish case of Rock Cemetery in Caernarvon Township, Pennsylvania.

For years, friends and family members had been visiting their loved ones at Rock Cemetery. Local resident Barbara Miller had come nearly every Sunday to be with her three-year-old child Ricky, who died of brain tumors in 1980. And for years, eighty-seven-year-old Hazel Hamm had been visiting the gravesite of her husband, Doug. Hazel had purchased a tombstone and gravesite next to Doug's, where she planned to rest in peace someday.

Rock Cemetery, like any cemetery in America, is a place where people go to pay their respects, to grieve, to be alone in a quiet place. Cemeteries are public places where we go to carry out some of our most sacred cultural rituals. We bury our loved ones beneath the ground and formally say good-bye. We see grass growing and flowers blooming, and we have to admit that life goes on. We return to remember, to think of the good times, to experience the sweet catharsis of grief. As gloomy as cemeteries may be, we have them because, ultimately, they make our lives more livable.

So you can imagine just how shocking it was for Hazel, Barbara, and many other locals when newcomers Paul and Jean Dovin bought a plot of land that included Rock Cemetery and posted "No Trespassing" signs around it. The new landowners made it known that police would be called if trespassers entered the cemetery. All visits, burials, flowers, and flags were banned. The Dovins decided to permit access to visitors only for the purpose of exhuming family members so that the bodies could be moved to another cemetery.[29]

"It just makes me sick to my stomach," Hazel Hamm told the local TV station. "I want to be buried beside [my husband], and I think I have a right to be."

Referring to having to rebury her son, Barbara Miller said, "I don't think I can go through all that again. What's wrong with these people?"[30]

The closing of Rock Cemetery is an extraordinary case, but closing down public places in America is hardly out of the ordinary. For decades, property owners across America have been closing off access to their private land, which they previously allowed the public access to—our favorite swimming holes, beaches, fields, and forests. What were once the special places we had visited to enjoy solitude, nature, or a good hike became exclusively owned by one or two (usually privileged) property owners.*

Let's start in Hawaii. On the island of Kauai, Facebook CEO and billionaire Mark Zuckerberg bought seven hundred acres of beachfront property and immediately built a six-foot wall around it. Hundreds of Hawaiians claimed ancestral rights to Zuckerberg's vacation grounds under the Kuleana Act of 1850, which gives rights—including the right of family members to roam over the land—to natives who live on the land.[31] The area being claimed amounted to only eight acres out of Zuckerberg's seven hundred, but he decided to sue hundreds of Hawaiians anyway. Zuckerberg's neighbors called his wall, which now blocks views of the ocean, a "monstrosity."[32]

Zuckerberg's wall made national headlines, but most of the time the stories of these closures are briefly noted in local newspapers, as in the case of a natural spring in Kentucky. For decades, families in Laurel County, Kentucky, had been drawing water from a spring so they could have clean and fresh water for drinking, canning vegetables, and making baby formula.[33] This community tradition ended when the spring was bought and closed off by the Nature Conservancy.

In the summer of 2016, in Saugerties, New York, officers issued more than 100 trespassing tickets and 150 parking tickets. They began arresting people for swimming in what was ranked as one of the top

---

* It should be said that the many forthcoming examples of places that have been closed off are a select handful gathered from news stories between 2014 and the first half of 2016.

swimming holes in the country. After a forecast for an especially hot summer day, Police Chief Joseph Sinagra told reporters, "I guarantee we'll be up there tomorrow arresting people."[34]

Sometimes these closures prevent people from visiting places of historic importance, as in the Killdeer Mountains of North Dakota, where a pair of property owners closed off access to a "medicine hole" holy site that figures into Sioux and Hidatsa legends—a spot of land that also offers a panoramic view of the 1864 Killdeer Mountain Battlefield.[35]

Because hiking trails often cross many landowners' properties, trails are at risk of being severed if a landowner decides she no longer wants people walking on her land. In Winston-Salem, North Carolina, a homeowner association closed off a popular section of greenway that connected a public bridge with another public greenway.[36] In Duluth, Minnesota, one landowner forced a major reroute of the more than three-hundred-mile Superior Hiking Trail because he decided to discontinue allowing hikers on it.[37] Around Avila Beach in California, a pair of property owners who bought a thirty-seven-acre property that overlooked Pirate's Cove decided to place fences and gates around a popular trail.[38] In Lancaster County, Pennsylvania, Talen Energy closed off access to four hundred acres of newly bought land that included a park, an arboretum, picnic pavilions, a baseball diamond, and the trailheads of several trails that featured the yearly ten-mile Conestoga Trail Run.[39]

Often owned by rich beachfront property owners, America's coastlines are especially at risk of being closed off to the public. Coastal states typically acknowledge the public's right to access coasts, but the reality is much different. Florida's constitution says that the public has the right to the high-tide mark, but 60 percent of Florida's beaches are private and generally inaccessible, according to the Florida Department of Environmental Protection in 2005.[40] In Clearwater, Florida, for instance, homeowners with million-dollar beachfront property roped off sections of beach.[41]

Public beaches controlled by private owners are not just a problem for Florida. It's a problem along most of our coastlines. In Harpswell, Maine, property owners closed off a private road that had been used by the public to get to the beach. (Now the only way to legally get to the beach is to take a boat, the Maine Supreme Judicial Court ruled.[42]) In Seattle, Washington, property owners closed off access to a beach that had been used for eighty-two years. A local, Kevin Hendrickson, said that he'd taken his yellow lab Stella on daily walks to the beach, but that now "she just sits there and stares at the fence."[43] In Hampton, Virginia, the Virginia Supreme Court ruled that one landowner could keep his neighbors off the beach because the easement on his property, which people used to walk along, got submerged by the Chesapeake Bay.[44] In Milford, Connecticut, a landowner with a million-dollar property of .2 acres closed off access to the Atlantic Ocean.[45] In Malibu, California, property owners post illegitimate "No Parking" and "No Trespassing" signs around the Pacific. In another Malibu incident, the Paradise Cove Land Company, which runs a restaurant, sold illegal twenty-dollar-a-day "beach club membership fees" for beachfront access.[46] In Rye, New Hampshire, the owner of Wentworth by the Sea Country Club, a private golf course, tried to ban access to what he thought was his own private oceanfront.[47] In Westerly, Rhode Island, a Superior Court judge ruled that it was okay for landowners to close off two miles of oceanfront beach with "No Trespassing" signs and snow fencing.[48] In Honolulu, Hawaii, a pair of homeowners lined a public causeway with boulders and put up "No Trespassing" signs.[49] Also in Hawaii, the public has access up to the vegetation line, but landowners in recent years have planted vegetation farther *makai* (or seaward) so that landowners can build closer to the ocean.[50] In Sea Bright, New Jersey, six private beach clubs cut off access to the state-owned seawall and taxpayer-funded wooden staircases.[51] On Martha's Vineyard in Massachusetts (an affluent area not known for theft or vandalism), a homeowner posts a "Guard Dogs on Duty" sign along his stretch of beach and pays a private security guard to check for people's fishing licenses. (In Massachusetts, citizens have the right to use the beach, but only in the cases of "fishing, fowling, and navigating," so people must carry a fishing rod and license to enjoy a simple stroll.)[52] Near San Francisco, California, Vinod Khosla, a Silicon Valley billionaire, bought a $32.5 million 89-acre beachfront property, which he closed off to the public, including a number of surfers who had been using the beach for decades. Charitably, Mr. Khosla offered to reopen the road to the beach—for the price of $30 million, to be paid by California taxpayers.[53]

Essentially all coastal states allow residents to walk along the wet sand of their coasts, though the states of Delaware, Maine, Massachusetts, Pennsylvania, and Virginia use the mean low-tide line to mark the edge of a landowner's property. In some of these states, the landowner owns all the way down to the water at low tide. In Maine, Massachusetts, and Virginia, the coasts are mostly privately owned, according to the Surfrider Foundation.[54]

The larger problem isn't whether or not you're allowed to walk along the beach; the larger problem is how to get to the beach in the first place. Many beach towns discourage outsiders from using beaches by purposefully neglecting to provide spots where people can reach the beaches by road or over public property. Many towns, in fact, restrict parking anywhere near beach access routes, often by limiting parking to people who have parking permits issued by the local government.

Rivers and lakes are also at risk of being appropriated and closed off by the usual suspects: homeowner associations, affluent communities, and unwelcoming landowners. The lake filmed in the 1981 movie *On Golden Pond*, starring Henry Fonda and Katharine Hepburn, is called Squam Lake, and at almost 7,000 acres it's the second-biggest lake in New Hampshire. The lake itself is publicly owned, but for years the perimeter of Squam was privately owned and therefore inaccessible. Local Sydney Howe said that his neighbors were worried that "the great unwashed public will harm Squam." When the New Hampshire Fish and Game Department wanted to buy land to make the public lake accessible, a group of lakeside landowners got together and outbid the state so the lake could remain in private hands. During this period, local landowners would allow the public to access the lake, but requested "donations."[55] The landowners managed to keep the lake closed off to the public until 1999. As of today, there is one access point, according to the Squam Lakes Association.[56]

Joel Brammeier, the president and CEO of the Alliance for the Great Lakes, said that landowners have recently been organizing to restrict the historic access rights of the public. "Over the last twenty years, there has been a more organized effort by private coastal property owners around the Great Lakes to contest protected public uses of both public and private lands," said Brammeier. "For a long time beach access was a quiet area in Great Lakes law, but that's changed because of private residential pressure and increased development." One such landowner organization around Lake Michigan is Save Our Shoreline. One of Save Our Shoreline's "ten objectives" is to keep the ordinary high water mark (which is where the public has historically been allowed to walk) at the water's edge. Defining the ordinary high water mark in this way would have the effect of limiting beach access and beach activities and weakening the public's rights. In Long Beach, Indiana, a property owner sued the state of Indiana, claiming that he had "complete and exclusive ownership" of a stretch of Lake Michigan waterfront and that no one had the right to swim, fish, sunbathe, or walk along his exclusive shore.[57] In Webster, New York, homeowners have banned visitors from Lake Ontario's shore. Apparently, people were using the "private sand" for activities as unthinkable as eating, drinking, cooking food, and walking dogs. Local owner Kristine Gilliam said she started off by walking down and saying, "Can I help you? Do you know somebody down here?" Gilliam determined, "We can't keep taking the nice approach anymore, and we can't allow this to continue."[58] In Johnston, Rhode Island, lakefront residents closed off public-access points to the Oak Swamp Reservoir. Mayor Joseph Polisena told access proponents, "There's nothing in your deed that says you have a right to get into that lake."[59] Despite there being few bodies of water in Nevada, in 2014 the Nevada Supreme Court ruled that Lake Tahoe beachfront owners are free to restrict access.[60] In Wisconsin Dells, Wisconsin, a learning center built a fence next to the Wisconsin River at a popular put-in site for kayakers and canoeists.[61] In the Adirondacks of New York, a landowner shut down access to a stream called Shingle Shanty Brook. Now paddlers are forced to endure a half-mile portage with their canoe to avoid using the navigable stream.[62] In 2015, New Mexico Governor Susana Martinez signed a bill into law that took away the public's right to walk over private land to get to public streams. These streams are the property of all of New Mexico's residents, but now, if a landowner has a stream going through his land, the landowner can effectively ban the rest of the state of New Mexico from the stream.[63] In other words, the stream is public, but the access to it is now private.

Again, these examples are just a select handful gathered from news articles from a two-and-a-half-year period, between 2014 and the first half of 2016. Let's not forget all the other places that have been closed off in the past 150 years. Let's not forget about all of the little rights of way, footpaths, and special spots that have been closed off but never made the local news and can't be found on Google. I have one such place: a woodland walk near a friend's home where I've spent a significant amount of time over the past seven years. Once a week or so, I'd go on a walk down the gravel road that meanders through the woods around a few large boulders. The road leads to the top of a forested ridge, where I'd sit on a rusty park bench for a few minutes before heading back down toward home. A new property owner, who bought land on the ridge and considered that part of the road his own, spray-painted purple rings around the trees lining the road and closed off the road with a gate. Hanging on the gate is a wooden cutout of an assault rifle painted black. When I first saw the gate and wooden rifle, I turned around and never went back. I didn't say anything to the new landowner because I didn't want to sour relations with a neighbor whom I'd have to live next to. Sadly, my response is probably typical among folks who lose access to their favorite places.

Placing public lands in private hands

For decades, a number of states out West have been dealing with the closing off of not just *private* land but also *public* land. In some cases, our publicly owned national forests and Bureau of Land Management lands (often just as scenic as our most celebrated national parks) are the exclusive pleasures of a few fortunate property owners. John Gibson, the president of the Public Land/Water Access Association, said, "For over two decades we've seen some people work to privatize our public lands by cutting off public access. And once somebody controls the access, they control all the public resources, including fish and wildlife on those lands."[64] In other words, when our public lands are surrounded by private property, there's no way in, except for the few lucky property owners who live next to our public lands. Many of these landowners financially benefit by closing off public lands because they can charge hunters large sums of money for hunting privileges over their land and the adjoining public lands. On three occasions, Gibson and his organization sued James Cox Kennedy, a software billionaire from Atlanta, Georgia, who kept closing down public roads in Montana so he could have the public land for himself. "They like to buy it right on the boundary of the national forests, so there's no chance of people getting into there," said Gibson about outsiders coming into Montana and securing public land for themselves. The problem isn't always outsiders, either. "The Montana landowner," said Gibson, "knows his land is worth more if it has no public access through it, so he will close off the old road if he can because he can sell his land for more money to one of these outsiders."

Of course access isn't just Montana's problem. The BLM says that about 9 percent of its lands, or twenty-three million acres, are inadequately accessible because of private land.[65] Many of our Forest Service lands and Fish and Wildlife lands are inaccessible, too, but I'll talk more about that in Chapter 6.

Access was passionately debated in Montana before the 2016 gubernatorial election because Republican candidate Greg Gianforte (the politician who would, in a later congressional campaign in 2017, assault a reporter for asking a question) had sued

Montana Fish, Wildlife & Parks over an easement on his property near Bozeman. He is on the record saying that Montana Fish, Wildlife & Parks is "at war" with property owners because they're trying to "extract access and using extortion to do it."[66]

In Washington State, the Weyerhaeuser timber company, which owns thirteen million acres[67] across the United States, began charging fees to enter woodlands. They charge $300 for motorized access for a year, which covers the cost of your family, but if you take three unrelated friends, the cost for one vehicle would be $1,200.[68] (Nonmotorized access costs $50 for a yearly pass.) Sixty miles north of Los Angeles is the 270,000-acre Tejon Ranch, the largest plot of contiguous private property in California, where landowners charge the public for access. For five months a year, members pay $2,500 to get a key to the ranch gates and access to twenty-five thousand acres of prime California golden hilly grasslands.[69]

Charging for access isn't necessarily new. Hunters have long been paying for access, but there aren't many examples of companies forcing you to pay simply to hike. Could this sort of transaction be the future of recreation in America? The threat of losing precious public lands to private hands is real. Consider the Sagebrush Rebellion, which has been brewing out West for decades.

The "rebellion" began in the 1970s and 1980s when people in western states began protesting the large amount of land owned by the federal government out West, which they thought was getting in the way of their economic development, usually in the form of ranching, oil, or mining. In 1980, while on the campaign trail, Ronald Reagan said, "I happen to be one who cheers and supports the Sagebrush Rebellion. Count me in as a rebel."[70]

In recent years, the Sagebrush Rebellion has been a front-page story twice. The first was in 2014, when Nevada rancher Cliven Bundy instigated what became known as the Bundy standoff. For decades, Bundy refused to pay fees for grazing his cattle on federal property, amounting to more than $1 million in unpaid fees. After the BLM rounded up his trespassing cattle, three hundred people, many of whom were militiamen and anti-government ideologues, joined Bundy in an armed protest that briefly made him a media darling on right-wing news programs until his racist comments got to be too much. (Bundy had wondered aloud if "the negro" would have been better off remaining in slavery.)

Two years later, Bundy's sons would go a step further and occupy a federal building in Oregon. Cliven's son Ammon Bundy was responding to the imprisonment of two Oregon ranchers, Dwight and Steve Hammond, who had both served a year and three months for arson on federal lands. The Hammonds were resentenced to five years, which inflamed Ammon, his brother Ryan, and other ranchers and militiamen, who took over the headquarters of the Malheur National Wildlife Refuge. It was a symbolic occupation of federal property, which they hoped would spark a movement to end what they saw as government overreach. "We are using the wildlife refuge as a place for individuals across the United States to come and assist in helping the people of Harney County claim back their lands and resources," Ammon Bundy said.

The Bundys are associated with several movements, including the Sagebrush Rebellion, the sovereign citizens movement (which rejects federal authority), and the Mormon Constitutionalist movement. Mormon Constitutionalists consider the Constitution a divine document (one that was written by Jesus, according to Cliven Bundy). Some Mormon Constitutionalists believe in the "White Horse Prophecy," which was given to Joseph Smith and which predicts a time when the Constitution will "hang by a thread" and must be preserved by Mormons to rescue America from doom. For an understanding of the occupiers' worldview, one need look no further than the writing of Ryan Bundy, who calls himself the "seed of Abram" and who outlined his views in a written court statement, which he used to try to delegitimize court proceedings since he believes the court holds no authority over a sovereign citizen such as himself. "I rule over the fish of the sea and the birds of the air, over the livestock, *over all the earth*, and over all the creatures that move along the ground," wrote Ryan Bundy, echoing Genesis 1:29–30 and Moses 2:26–30. "I believe God gave I every seed-bearing plant on the face of the whole earth and every tree that has fruit with seed in it, as well as all the beasts of the earth and all the birds of the air and all the creatures that move on the ground—everything that has the breath of life in it; I am without evidence to the contrary, therefore it is so."[71] A grounding in the fringe beliefs of Mormon theology, an Old Testament understanding of ecology and land ownership, a misunderstanding of the history of the West (more on this soon), and our own unique twenty-first-century brand of

paranoid alt-right conservatism were the ideological
influences that would make the Bundys bold enough
to take over a harmless wildlife refuge. But behind
the waving flags and pious pronouncements of liberation, let's call this occupation what it was: "the
same old land lust" by "another gang of armed and
desperate white riff-raff," writes Anthony McCann
for the *LA Review of Books*.[*][72]

The occupiers used a boat launch area for fire-
arms training (where 1,685 spent shell casings were
found), looted the headquarters, and used a government excavator to expand a parking lot. After a pipe
broke, officials reported that the occupiers defe-
cated "everywhere," and investigators later found
"significant amounts of human feces" near sacred
Indian artifacts.[73]

The Bundys believed they were heroically claiming back Americans' land, but their understanding
of American history was more than a little facile.
According to the Bundy ranch website, the Bundys
believe that Teddy Roosevelt kicked ranchers out of
the present-day area of the refuge to create an "Indian reservation (without Indians)." The Indians
spoken of—the Paiute—have a different understanding of local history.

The Paiute wandered across the Great Basin in
the Oregon area for millennia, following a pattern
of seasonal movements from the basin to the mountains and back again. When settlers arrived, the
story that unfolded is typical for native peoples

---

* Special credit goes to McCann's wonderful reporting
on the Malheur occupation, which has been my key source
on the occupation in this chapter.

across America: first a period of disease, then massacres at the hands of white Americans, then stalwart resistance, and finally tragic submission. In 1879, 350 Paiute endured a forced relocation to the Malheur Indian Reservation, a 350-mile march through snow and bitter cold, remembered as the Paiute "Trail of Tears."[74]

The tragedy, though, does not end there. As more and more white ranchers settled in the area, the newcomers wanted to dismantle the reservation. A corrupt and hostile government agent took control of the reservation. The Paiute were starving and fled for the mountains.

When the Paiute history was shared with Ammon, Ammon said, "That's interesting, I don't know anything about that. But they deserve to be free too." His brother Ryan was less forgiving. Despite Ryan Bundy's penchant for zany ideologies and harebrained religion, he suddenly became rigidly and menacingly practical when it came to the rights of native peoples. The Paiute "had the claim to the land, but they lost that claim," Ryan Bundy said. "The current culture is the most important."

The presence of armed white ranchers seizing land to give it back to other white people was an unpleasant history pageant for the Paiute to have to watch. The Paiute fiercely opposed the occupation and refused to acknowledge or meet with the occupiers, despite a number of seemingly earnest overtures.

The occupiers began rummaging through boxes of Paiute artifacts in the basement of the headquarters. Some of these boxes had been damaged and were neglected by the Fish and Wildlife Service, which the occupiers used to add more fuel to their anti-government fires. They also thought returning these boxes to the recalcitrant Paiute might help win their support. In a video, occupier LaVoy Finicum calls for opening up dialogue with the Paiute, and occupier Blaine Cooper calls for rightful owners to "come back and claim their belongings."

The occupiers here betray their ignorance of how the Paiute understand property. The Paiute don't have the absolute "that is yours" and "this is mine" understanding of private property that most all Americans do. Even Cooper's terms *rightful* and *owner*—though perfectly ordinary and noncontroversial to an American such as myself—are not applicable to the Paiute understanding of property. To the Paiute, land is more than just a piece of earth to be divided into individualized parcels to be exploited, developed, or conserved. "It's more like family than property," said Diane Teeman, the archaeologist for the tribe, about the Paiute's relationship with the land. And because the land is like family, it cannot be owned, just as you cannot own an uncle. "All the dirt I dig up in my garden," Teeman said, "my ancestors are woven through that, and that land is woven through me."

According to the Paiute, when we do something to the land, we're doing something to all the people that came before us. When a Paiute finds an artifact in the land, they "bless it, say a prayer, or sing, sprinkle some tobacco or sage on it, and return it to the earth," said Jarvis Kennedy, a Tribal Council member. "Because it's ours but not ours. I think that's hard for people to understand."

For good reason, the Paiute were alarmed when they saw Finicum on YouTube rummaging around the boxes of artifacts. That evening, Finicum was shot and killed while resisting arrest. "We don't think it's a coincidence that he died," Kennedy said. "No disrespect. We feel for his family. We didn't want that to happen to him. But you can't go messing with objects like that without protection."

In the end, the occupation was a failure. Dozens were arrested. Finicum was dead. The droves of land-hungry Americans never answered Ammon's call. Replacing stolen or damaged equipment would cost taxpayers $1.7 million. Feces were everywhere.

Mostly, the occupiers were either ignored or ridiculed. On Twitter, people tweeted fan fiction of the occupiers under the hashtag #BundyEroticFanFic. The occupiers had no problem remembering to bring an abundance of guns and ammo, but, despite supposedly being self-sufficient outdoorsmen, they forgot to bring food for a long occupation. They turned to Facebook for help, calling for sympathizers to send "snacks,"[75] to which the public responded with more ridicule and gummy snacks in the shape of penises. In one popular YouTube video, an occupier showed a series of "gifts" the occupiers received, including a long dildo and other anatomically correct candies. Living in their bubble of militiamen and extremists, the occupiers failed to realize that most of the American public do not share their concerns about the size of our federal estate or about having to pay reasonable fees for grazing rights on public lands.[76] The locals turned against the occupiers, and even the Hammond family never came out in support of the occupation.

It may seem as though the government, conservationists, and Twitter got the last laugh, but the

Sagebrush Rebellion rolls on. The Bundys and company were acquitted in October 2016. At the same time in North Dakota, Native Americans, who were opposing the Dakota Access Pipeline to safeguard the climate, their water, and the land with its mystic swirl of stories, ancestors, and animals, were being arrested and brutally treated by a militarized police force. The Bundys may ultimately have lost their standoff and occupation, and they may have been caricatured as extremists in the media, but their cause is alive and well, now carried on by suit-and-tie corporate lobbyists and politicians in state legislatures and the US Congress.

In 2015, Senate Amendment 838 passed through the US Senate, calling for "the disposal of certain Federal land," which includes refuges, national forests, and public wilderness.[77] Three other bills (House Resolutions 3650, 2316, and 4579) advanced out of committee in the House, allowing individual states to undermine wilderness designations, to hand over management duties of federal lands to a few Utah counties, and to claim two million acres of national forest lands for themselves so long as they prioritize logging.[78] The House of Representatives' 2015 budget resolution supported "reducing the Federal estate, and giving States and localities more control over the resources within their boundaries. This will lead to increased resource production and allow States and localities to take advantage of the benefits of increased economic activity."[79] Senator Ted Cruz, who was runner-up to Donald Trump in the 2016 Republican primaries, called for an amendment that would make the federal government sell off a substantial amount of its lands to states and to the highest-bidding private citizens.[80] "Two percent of [Texas] is owned by the federal government," Cruz said about his home state. "I gotta tell you, in Texas, that's two percent too much."[81]

There have been more than fifty bills in state legislatures in recent years to seize federal lands.[82] The Wilderness Society has counted nineteen states (not all of them Western) that strive to place public lands into private hands.[83] In 2012, Utah passed the Transfer of Public Lands Act, which was signed by Governor Gary Herbert. This act called for the Forest Service, which owns 15 percent of Utah land, and the Bureau of Land Management, which owns 42 percent, to hand over these public lands to the state of Utah. Inspired by Utah, between 2012 and 2013 Wyoming, Nevada, Idaho, Montana, and New Mexico passed similar bills or resolutions.

Let's not kid ourselves into thinking that these states are going to use these public lands for the public good. Budgeting money to manage these newly acquired lands would be a big problem for these states. David Garbett, a staff lawyer with the nonprofit Southern Utah Wilderness Alliance, said, "If Utah is successful in its quest, the real losers will be the public. The only way the Utah legislature can generate money from the public lands is to ramp up development and hold a fire sale to clear inventory. That means that the places the public has come to know and love will be sold to the highest bidder and barricaded with 'No Trespassing' signs."[84]

Western states already have sold off 31 million acres of state land. Idaho, since 2010, has sold 100,000 acres.[85] At one auction in 2016, Utah sold more than 3,600 acres for $6.2 million. A total of

391 acres of Comb Ridge—a magnificent and ar-
chaeologically significant sandstone monocline
within the borders of the Bears Ears National
Monument[86]—was sold to the Lyman Family Farm,
Inc. for $500,000. The new landowners immediately
blocked a county road, which closed off access to
the people of Bluff, Utah,[87] who had used the area
for hiking after work.[88] Josh Ewing, the executive
director of Friends of Cedar Mesa, called the purchase a cautionary tale. "I think this is an illustration
of what would happen if the states got hold of all
those [federal] lands," said Ewing. "They would sell
them off to the highest bidder."

When America's land is not being seized one
swimming hole, one trail, one coastline, and one
cemetery at a time, these greater forces—whether
they be radical ranchers, the super rich, or the US
Congress and state legislatures—threaten wide ex-
panses of our public lands. The closing of America
fits a larger trend that has long been developing—a
trend of privatizing America, of reducing the role
of government, and of giving lands, powers, and
breaks to the wealthiest of us.

It's not all bad news, though. Even though he's
currently a congressman, Greg Gianforte lost his
previous campaign for governor in 2016 to Steve
Bullock, a champion of public-access rights. John
Gibson, the president of the Public Land/Water
Access Association, continues to win court battles
against rich landowners in Montana who are opposed to public access. The Honolulu sign erectors
were forced to pull them down. In Indiana, the court
ruled for greater public access to Lake Michigan.
In California, they have passed a law that fines

beachfront homeowners who put up illegitimate "Keep Out" signs.[89] All over the country, groups big and small have taken their grievances to Facebook and town halls to fight for access to their favorite places.

But America, nevertheless, continues to be shut down. While a state politician has tried to fight for access to Rock Cemetery in Caernarvon Township, Pennsylvania, residents like Barbara Miller and Hazel Hamm are still barred from visiting the graves of loved ones. The Sagebrush Rebellion rolls on, and legislators continue to call for the privatization of public lands. Great stretches of our coastlines and lakes are off-limits to millions of people. Trails are still being severed. Swimming holes are still being barricaded. And the rights of the public are still being taken away for the exclusive pleasures of a handful of landowners.

In the summer of 2017, New Jersey Governor Chris Christie ordered Island Beach State Park to be closed to the public during a budget standoff. Christie and his family had the gall to sunbathe on the empty beach, as if it were their own private property. Newsmen took aerial photographs of Christie in his bathing suit, and a scandal followed. Here we have a prime example of the rich and privileged using public land as their own personal playground. Except, in this case, it ended as it should have: Christie was properly chastised, and soon after the scandal the public was welcomed back onto the beach, just in time for the July Fourth weekend.[90]

Most times, though, these lands quietly slip from the public's grasp, never to be retrieved again. Maybe, for a day, these closures are chronicled in the local newspaper or they are remembered by the dispossessed. But their beauties and pleasures will remain unknown to subsequent generations. These are our lost landscapes, banished from our memory, excised from our consciousness.

In early twenty-first-century America, this land is clearly not our land.

CHAPTER 3

A Brief History of Trespassing

There is nothing which so generally strikes the imagination, and engages the affections of mankind, as the right of property; or that sole and despotic dominion which one man claims and exercises over the external things of the world, in total exclusion of the right of any other individual in the universe.

—William Blackstone, *Commentaries on the Laws of England (1765–1769)*[91]

When we think of the twentieth century's most historic acts of civil disobedience, we tend to think of the sit-ins, the freedom rides, the protest marches. We don't think of the trespasses over wild land, which happen to be a style of disobedience that nobody has mastered more than the English. And of all of England's great trespasses, none has been as romanticized, as controversial, and perhaps as influential as the 1932 mass trespass of Kinder Scout.

In the heart of Northern England, between the cities of Manchester and Sheffield, is a forty-mile-wide stretch of sparsely populated hill country, now part of a protected area known as the Peak District. To the eye of any experienced hill walker, the Peak District is exquisite hiking terrain. The valley, carpeted with well-watered pasture and dotted with cotton balls of sheep, is surrounded by steep hills, out of which sprout copses of beech, field maple, and English oak. The peaks, a far cry from the stone pinnacles of our Rockies, are more like gentle plateaus—not to be conquered with crampons and climbing ropes but to be rambled over with hiking boots and walking sticks. The biggest of them is Kinder Scout, a 2,087-foot hump of heather whose windswept top rises above the valley's morning fog, which when dissolved by sunshine unveils a summer landscape of purple bell heather and yellow eyebright flowers that buzz with bilberry bumblebees. It is one of England's grandest landscapes, and for years it was off-limits to everyone but a few aristocrats.

Starting in the 1400s, the English aristocracy began seizing commoners' homes to make this land their own—a process known as "enclosure." (It's called "enclosure" because the land would be enclosed by a hedge or wall, often for the purposes of intensive farming, grazing, or securing grouse and deer populations for sport hunting.) Between 1760 and 1870, a sixth of England, as a result of nearly four thousand acts of Parliament, was transformed from communal land into enclosed private property. The enclosure bill of 1869, for example, set aside three acres for recreation out of 6,916 acres of soon-to-be-enclosed land.[92] In 1815, Parliament had given power to magistrates to shut down walking paths they considered unnecessary.[93]

In the Peak District, Lord Howard in 1821 closed off an old Roman right of way with padlocks and "No Road" signs that ran along the base of Kinder Scout. In 1836, an act of enclosure turned over the Peak District, which was "king's land" (or public land), to a handful of rich landowners, mostly the 9th Duke of Devonshire. Of the Peak District's 150,000 acres, only 1,200 (less than 1 percent) were open to public access.[94] These places weren't just enclosed by harmless "No Trespassing" signs and hedgerows. Gamekeepers were hired and armed with guns and sticks, and they were said to prey on solitary walkers. They even used telescopes to identify trespassers from afar.[95] Over the years, walkers were able to regain some of their walking grounds, but Kinder Scout remained "the forbidden mountain."

The landowners who owned these vast personal pleasure grounds were the same people who owned the squalid factories in which all these hill walkers worked. In 1932, Benny Rothman, a twenty-year-old self-educated auto mechanic, said, "We ramblers, after a hard week's work in smoky towns and cities, go out rambling for relaxation, a breath of fresh air, a little sunshine. But we find when we go out that the finest rambling country is closed to us, just because certain individuals wish to shoot for about ten days a year."

As workers fought for and won their eight-hour days and five-day workweeks, they could then focus on "securing space in which to enjoy this hard-won time," wrote Rebecca Solnit in *Wanderlust*. Rambling clubs sprang up across the country, and in 1932, almost one hundred years after the Peak District had been given over to aristocrats, several of these groups set their sights on Kinder Scout. If it was going to be taken from them by law, they were going to seize it back by foot.

Four hundred ramblers, men and women, most of them under twenty-one years of age,[96] clad in old army tops, multicolored sweaters, khaki shorts, and worn work boots (the standard hiking garb of the day), carrying enormous rucksacks (because carrying full packs was the "done thing" at the time), showed up in the town of Hayfield and made their way toward the broad gritstone peak. On their climb, twenty to thirty gamekeepers emerged, threatening, shouting, and, one can imagine, wagging their dreaded sticks at the approaching crowd of walkers. What happened next would spark a firestorm of controversy and set in motion changes that would transform how England thinks about private property.

———

The mass trespass of Kinder Scout is an example of what happens when two groups of people with entirely different notions of property clash. In this case, one side attempted to literally guard the existing system of absolute private property, while the other ignored that system and showcased their own—a notion of private property that was flexible enough to allow public access for purposes of recreation.

Property is not a law of physics that is consistent, inevitable, and universal, like gravity. Property, rather, is cultural. Societies have differing systems of property the same way societies have distinct styles of clothing and music. Lenin's Soviet Union believed that all property should be owned by the state.

Jefferson's United States believed that property should be owned mostly by individual citizens. And many hunter-gatherer societies believed that the earth could not be possessed. And as we saw with the Kinder Scout trespassers, there are sometimes heretics within societies who speak out against their society's dominant system of property.

"No man made the land," said English philosopher John Stuart Mill in his *Principles of Political Economy* in 1848. "It is the original inheritance of the whole species . . . The land of every country belongs to the people of that country." When Mill said that "no man made the land," he was challenging the prevailing notion that private property is a sacred, timeless, and universal institution. Mill seems to believe that the authority behind private property does not come from God, religious texts, or some universal fact of human nature.

Private property is merely an idea. A mere mortal's idea. And Mill's idea that the land "belongs to the people of that country" is just that: another idea.

Mill wasn't alone in sharing heretical ideas about private property. Henry David Thoreau, in his 1862 essay "Walking," worried about the day when a few American property owners might "take a narrow and exclusive pleasure" in their property, which would convert walking into "trespassing on some gentleman's grounds." American economist Henry George (1839–1897) said that "private property in land is a bold, bare, enormous wrong, like that of chattel slavery . . . [T]he equal right of all men to the use of land is as clear as their equal right to breathe the air—it is a right proclaimed by the fact of their existence."[97] Jean-Jacques Rousseau (1712–1778) yelled out, "You are lost if you forget that the fruits belong to all and the earth to no one!"[98]

Plato (approx. 428–347 BCE) may be one of history's earliest champions of shared property. Plato lived during a time when the Greek city-states were in a constant state of turmoil. He was inspired by the history of Sparta, where a highly centralized government had prevented the concentration of wealth, promoted an egalitarian society, and rejected the notion of private property (everything from material goods to a man's wife and children). Sparta, according to Plato, was a shining example of stability, far removed from the bribery, greed, and ambition that troubled his native Athens.[99] The lessons of Spartan history would shape Plato's utopia, which he described in his *Republic* and *Laws*. He imagined a state run by wise men called Guardians who would possess no lands and would therefore have no reason to "tear the city in pieces by differing about 'mine' and 'not mine.'" In *Laws*, he backed away from some of his more radical ideas, such as abolishing the family, but he still called for a highly centralized society, where citizens could not enlarge their holdings by buying land or participating in a range of profit-making enterprises. He believed that produce should be distributed equally to slaves, citizens, and artisans.[100] "The first and highest form of the State," Plato wrote, "and of the government and of the law is that in which there prevails most widely the ancient saying, that 'Friends have all things in common.'"[101]

Plato's student Aristotle (384–322 BCE), on the other hand, may be antiquity's earliest known advocate of private property. In *Politics*, Aristotle claimed that collective ownership creates an atmosphere of neglect because "everybody is more inclined to neglect the duty which he expects another to fulfill."[102] But Aristotle does not suggest that everyone should be allowed to greedily hoard his possessions. "Better that property should be private, but the use of it common," he wrote. Aristotle called for private property, but a *shared* private property for reasons of efficiency, productivity, and social harmony.

Up until recent times, on most places on earth, personal ownership of land was an odd, if inconceivable, notion. In feudal Europe, only lords owned land, which was actually owned by monarchs, who actually got their authority from divine law. ("Owned" probably isn't even the right word to use because the lord had to meet the complex set of religious, governmental, and moral obligations that came with land ownership.)

In indigenous communities around the globe, personal ownership of large pieces of land was unheard of. There are countless examples of Native North Americans referring to the earth as an unownable entity. Chief Crowfoot of the Siksika, a tribe based in what is now Alberta, Canada, said in the nineteenth century that land "was put there by the Great Spirit and we cannot sell it because it does not really belong to us."[103] Massasoit, a Wampanoag tribal leader who dealt with the pilgrims and whose people came from what are now Rhode Island and southeastern Massachusetts, said, "The land is our mother nourishing all her children, beasts, birds, fish, and all men. The woods, the streams, everything on it belongs to everybody and is for the use of all. How can one man say it belongs only to him?"[104] Karl Marx was inspired by many communal societies, especially the Irish, whose Brehon laws outlined a sophisticated system of communal ownership that lasted until 1600. With these early societies in mind, he and Friedrich Engels argued for the abolition of private property in *The Communist Manifesto*.[105]

Despite the many voices calling for a communal style of land ownership, the world has come to be dominated by private property. Thomas Jefferson is considered America's architect of private property. Jefferson believed that small landholdings gave citizens economic security, encouraged independent political judgment, and promoted Republican virtues.*[106] In Jefferson's view, the more people who owned land, the better. He imagined a nation of sturdy, independent farmers, and his vision influenced federal land distribution policies, such as the Northwest Ordinance in 1787 and the Homestead Act of 1862, the latter of which gave homesteaders their own 160-acre section of land.[107] Jefferson drew from the work of English philosopher John Locke (1632–1704), who said in his *Two Treatises of Government* that the earth is unowned or held in common until a person mixes his labor with it. Then the labored land becomes someone's private property. In other words, the earth is unowned and held in common until someone starts grazing cattle, chopping

---

* Jefferson said as much in a letter to John Jay in 1785: "Cultivators of the earth are the most valuable citizens. They are the most vigorous, the most independent, the most virtuous, and they are tied to their country and wedded to its liberty and interests by the most lasting bonds."[108]

down maples, or planting fields of turnips. Then the land on which these things are done becomes his and remains his until he dies or until he ceases mixing his labors with these lands.

Given Jefferson's place in history as architect of American private property, it may come as a surprise to learn that Jefferson was hardly the staunch advocate of private property in the ways we may imagine. Jefferson borrowed from Locke, but he disagreed with Locke's notion that private property originates when labor and the earth are mixed. Jefferson, rather, felt that property was something far simpler: It was a system created by law.[109] And, to Jefferson, private property was only worthwhile when it served the interests of ordinary citizens and the nation as a whole. While he was ambassador to France, he spoke with a poor French woman who lived on a few cents a day near a royal hunting park that she and the rest of her class were banned from. These huge private landholdings were owned by a handful of aristocrats, creating, as Jefferson put it in a letter to James Madison, an "enormous inequality producing so much misery to the bulk of mankind" that "legislators cannot invent too many devices for subdividing property."*

Jefferson was all for breaking up huge chunks of property owned by the rich, not to mention taxing

---

* Thomas Jefferson to James Madison, October 28, 1785: "Whenever there is in any country, uncultivated lands and unemployed poor, it is clear that the laws of property have been so far extended as to violate natural right. The earth is given as a common stock for man to labour and live on."[110]

land, and more radically, he even dabbled with thoughts of doing away with the system of wealth and land inheritance.[111] This was a man who, when listing our most precious and unalienable rights in the Declaration of Independence, cut out Locke's right of "estate" and put in its place the "pursuit of happiness."

Although Jefferson may indeed be the architect behind the world's most impressive experiment in private property, his original blueprints do not suggest that he would endorse the system we have today, in which the top hundred American landowners own nearly thirty-eight million acres[112] (equivalent to seventeen Yellowstone National Parks), and where someone like Facebook CEO and billionaire Mark Zuckerberg can erect a six-foot wall around his seven-hundred-acre Hawaiian beachfront property.[113]

———

It's one thing to quote the lofty ideals of high-minded philosophers, and it's another to take a look at the systems of property that have actually existed.

The written record goes back only five thousand years, but anthropologists who have studied hunter-gatherer societies have taught us that our species has, for most of our time on this planet, thought of property in a way that is far different from our thinking today. For these hunter-gatherer societies, the land was collectively owned, which suggests that our Paleolithic ancestors, for about two hundred thousand years, had the freedom to walk within their tribe's vast territories without worrying about getting fined for trespassing across a neighbor's yard. Often, these territories were huge. According to

Richard Pipes in *Property and Freedom*, in Tasmania in 1770 there were between two thousand and four thousand hunter-gatherers living on twenty-five thousand square miles of land, which means that, if distributed evenly, each citizen would have four thousand acres to herself.[114] According to calculations by Colin Clark and Margaret Haswell in *The Economics of Subsistence Agriculture*, a hunter-gatherer typically needs ten or more square miles for sustenance, whereas a farmer needs between half a square mile and three square miles. A farmer with domesticated animals needs a third of a square mile.[115] Of the three groups, the hunter-gatherer has, by far, the biggest playground.

But the Paleolithic was hardly a walker's paradise. Trespassing on another tribe's territory was a big no-no in many parts of the world. In *The World Until Yesterday*, author Jared Diamond describes how various traditional societies interpreted the concept of trespassing. In Alaskan Inupiat culture, trespassers from other tribes were routinely killed, even in cases in which seal hunters accidentally traveled from a drifting ice shelf onto another group's territory.[116] The Dani of western New Guinea's highlands patrolled precise borders and built thirty-foot-tall watchtowers to keep an eye out for trespassers.[117] But other groups have been far more inviting. The !Kung Bushmen of the Nyae Nyae area of the Kalahari Desert shared resources and open borders with neighboring tribes who could request permission to access lands.[118] In the Great Basin of modern-day Nevada, Utah, California, and Oregon, the Shoshone, with their sparse population densities, didn't have well-defined boundaries.[119]

But traveling outside of one's home territory, for many Paleolithic peoples, probably wasn't often necessary. In *The Third Chimpanzee,* Jared Diamond describes a team of American explorers who in 1938 discovered Stone Age tribes living in western Papua New Guinea. Not only were these New Guinea highlanders unaware of Western culture but their borders were so defined and traveling was so discouraged that the highlanders were even unaware of other nearby tribes. "For all but the last ten thousand years of human history, unfettered travel was impossible," said Diamond.

There were limits to where our hunter-gatherer ancestors could roam. Tribes more or less had sovereign borders. Individuals had special rights to certain places, like fishing holes. And there were firm rules of etiquette with respect to the privacy of individual dwellings. There were limits, but we as hunter-gatherers surely did not suffer from our modern-day nature deficit disorders. While the concept of "trespassing" very much existed—as it pertained to roaming beyond tribal boundaries—there is little to suggest that one was restrained from roaming *within* one's tribal boundaries. Perhaps there were restraints in the form of taboos and reasonable fears, but in these societies there certainly were neither barbed-wire fences nor "No Trespassing" signs. Nor were there guard dogs or the implicit understanding that you cannot walk on a particular flowery meadow because your neighbor Fred "owns" that land. Hunter-gatherers could roam to collect berries, hunt game, gather wood, explore terrain, and bless their gods and spirits in a far more uninhibited fashion than their private-propertied descendants.

One was not at risk of trespassing over a neighbor's vast property, because no one person owned a vast property.

———

The Neolithic Revolution marks the time frame when our species shifted from a hunter-gatherer way of life to an agricultural way of life. It began at different times in different places, but in the Fertile Crescent it began approximately twelve thousand years ago and would take shape over other continents during the next ten thousand years, until virtually the whole world's population was agricultural. With the advent of agriculture, populations became denser and new systems of property developed.

It's impossible to determine exactly when the supposed superiority of private property was first articulated. But from some of the earliest historical texts, we can see that the most advanced civilizations acknowledged and respected private property. The Code of Hammurabi (1750 BCE), a code of law for ancient Mesopotamia, mentions a number of property-related issues, including theft, slavery, land possession, animal possession, investments, and debts.[120]

Still, land that was unowned and shared was a fact of life for our farming and herding ancestors. It was even a prescribed system by almost all of the major religions. The Judeo-Christian tradition proclaims that nature is a "gift" (Genesis 9:1–3) and that "the profit of the land is for all" (Ecclesiastes 5:9).[121] In the Acts of the Apostles, people in Jerusalem "had all things common . . . Neither was there any among them that lacked: for as many as were possessors of lands or houses sold them." Augustine of Hippo said that common ownership would be the ideal condition in paradise, and Thomas Aquinas argued that everyone should get whatever they needed from their society's resources.[122] In Leviticus 23, Yahweh's commandment declares that "the land shall not be sold for ever: for the land is mine; for ye are strangers and sojourners with me."[123] Islam incorporated a similar view into Sharia law,[124] and Muhammad said that "the people are partners in three things: water, pastures, and fire." Hindus believed that "the soil is the common property of all," and nothing about Buddhists suggests that they were hoarders of land.[125]

While some cultures and religions championed shared property, as did many societies with animistic, nature-revering religions, our understanding of the land and its spirits and mystic potencies—common in hunter-gatherer societies—fell by the wayside as "population pressures [called] for a more rational method of exploitation," writes Richard Pipes in *Property and Freedom*.[126]

The commons

In spite of the emergence of private property, in the earliest stages of the private ownership of land, walking across land remained a daily part of life. In England and Wales, there are more than 130,000 miles of footpaths, many of which have been in existence for thousands of years.[127] Many of these paths are historic routes of communication and transportation between villages. People walked across fields to get from village to village, and from their homes to their churches, their cemeteries, their mills, their springs, and "the commons."

The commons were an integral part of medieval life for the ordinary villager. Although the king or a lord owned the land, peasants had rights: Cattle could graze in the commons, and peasants could cut lumber, draw water, collect peat, and use the commons for a number of purposes.[128] The commons were not places where individuals could exploit the land however they wished. Garrett Hardin, in his influential 1968 essay "The Tragedy of the Commons," asserted that collectively owned land is destined to be harmed because there will always be individuals within groups who act selfishly and who will consume more than their share of resources. In group communities, self-interest is indeed capable of depleting resources and devastating ecosystems, but the work of Nobel Prize winner Elinor Ostrom has shown that this isn't always the case. Ostrom has found that many people who share common lands (which she calls "common pool resources") are able to do so sustainably when community members can cooperate, trust one another, and act collectively. The commons, throughout history, have not all been slash-and-burn free-for-alls. The commons, writes Hartmut Zückert in *The Wealth of the Commons*, were often collectively managed by a community that appointed an assembly, a village mayor, and a village court to manage the land.[129] Although some citizens had more rights to the commons than others, artisans and laborers were permitted to use the land, and villages as a whole, at special times of the year, used the commons to dance, play cricket, race horses,[130] and celebrate folk customs, such as the annual procession around the commons' boundaries.[131] Marion Shoard, in *A Right to Roam*, described the English countryside before enclosure as "a busy theatre of constantly changing activities conducted by many different people."[132]

In 535 CE, Roman Emperor Justinian I gave the first legal recognition to the commons in the Institutes of Justinian, a code of laws that proclaimed:

> By the law of nature these things are common to mankind—the air, running water, the sea and consequently the shores of the sea . . . Also all rivers and ports are public, so that the right of fishing in a port and in rivers is common to all. And by the law of nations the use of the shore is also public, and in the same manner, the sea itself. The right of fishing in the sea from the shore belongs to all men.[133]

Rome would hold no power over this common property (*res communes*), which was different from public property (*res publicae*), which was public property owned by the state.[134] While there were real differences between the lives of slaves and citizens in Rome, Roman citizens were equals among each other, and Rome tried to live up to this ideal.

In the years after the fall of Rome, villagers across Europe retained their rights to the commons. In England, two years after the Magna Carta was signed, the Charter of the Forest was written in 1217, recognizing the rights of commoners to use what were then regarded as royal lands and forests.[135] Here, in the

Charter of the Forest, we see an oligarchical government acknowledging the people's right to their common lands. This acknowledgment shows just how embedded the commons were in medieval society. Throughout Medieval Europe, many people—despite being poor and powerless, relative to today's standards—still had rights to lands that were more or less their own.

Enclosing Britain

The English period of enclosure spanned centuries, starting around the second half of the sixteenth century.[136] Parliament justified enclosing land because it brought more land into production and improved efficiency. Enclosing land, writes historian J. M. Neeson, dealt with "the insubordination of commoners, the unimprovability of their pastures, and the brake on production represented by shared property."[137]

It was pointless for a commoner to hope for a "dim and distant Parliament of great landlords to come to his rescue,"[138] write authors J. L. and Barbara Hammond. Commoners stripped of their lands and rights were poorly compensated, if they were compensated at all. They were "surrounded by hether [sic] they dare not collect, and by a profusion of turnips they dare not pluck."[139] In the early 1600s, radical peasants who were called "levellers" and "diggers" destroyed ditches and fences that had been placed there by the enclosers.[140] There were riots and burnt fence posts, but these small revolts could not hold back a tidal wave of change.

In 1723, Prime Minister Robert Walpole introduced the Black Act to deal with peasants who resisted the enclosure movement. The rich wanted land for hunting lodges, fishponds, and deer populations. The "blacks" were peasant vigilantes who smeared their faces with soot to disguise themselves while illegally hunting wild game. The Black Act created fifty offenses that were punishable by death. Hundreds were executed, and after the act was repealed, offenders were shipped off to the Antipodes.[141]

Previously, people who walked across land would be considered travelers (or laborers, depending on the purpose of their journeys). Now, they were trespassers.

The end of enclosure and the "Ramblers movement"

Fields and woodlands were surrounded by man-made banks, ditches, and palisades.[142] Scottish hills were turned into vast deer parks. A few rich men claimed land that had been open for millennia, so that they could have parks of their own to hunt pheasants.[143] In 1824, Reverend Robert Slaney, who later would become a member of British Parliament representing Shrewsbury, said that the poor "have no place in which they may amuse themselves in summer evenings when the labour of the day is over, or when a holiday occurs."[144] When the Industrial Revolution spread across Britain, people in cities were living in "bug-ridden and verminous houses," wrote Benny Rothman, leader of the Kinder Scout trespass. "Not many had gardens, there were very few trees, shrubs, or flowers in the soul-destroying waste. The only way to enjoy a little fresh air and sunshine was to escape to the countryside."[145]

In response to the enclosures, groups sprang up across the country to fight for rights of way and footpaths. The earliest walking clubs included the Association for the Protection of Ancient Footpaths near York (1824) and another in Manchester (1826). Other clubs included the Association for the Protection of Public Rights of Roadway (1845), the Forest Ramblers' Club (formed by London businessmen in 1884), the Midlands Institute of Ramblers (formed by women teachers in 1894), the Manchester Rambling Club (1907), and the British Workers' Sports Federation (1928). There were many others.

By the 1930s, many of the walking groups were made up of working-class members who often had socialist sensibilities. But at the heart of all of these groups was a love for walking in nature and a belief in their right to walk the land. Kinder Scout trespasser Jimmy Jones of Manchester said, "We all supported the trespass because we were convinced that the land belonged to the people. It was in our blood."[146]

In 1932, the British Workers' Sports Federation sought to regain the lost moors of the Peak District. Their first attempt up Bleaklow Moor from the town of Glossop failed when ramblers ran into a gang of gamekeepers. It was clear that they needed more ramblers, so the trespassers publicized the mass trespass of Kinder Scout and found plenty of supporters from Manchester. The speaker who had been booked by the ramblers got cold feet, so Benny

Rothman, the twenty-year-old self-educated and unemployed auto mechanic, took the lead.

Rothman outsmarted the police (who had been waiting for him at the train station) by arriving by bicycle. Rothman led the way, and the ramblers sang while they outpaced the police up the mountain. Rothman may have been diminutive in size (he stood less than five feet tall), but he was a giant in spirit: He was a young man, bursting with passion and conviction, and at a quarry along the way, Rothman gave a rousing speech about the public-access movement. When the stick-wielding gamekeepers emerged, there was a brief scuffle, causing one of the gamekeepers to fall over and hurt his ankle. Still, the ramblers rambled on. Joined by other ramblers, who had taken a different route up the mountain from the town of Edale, the united group approached the peak and made Kinder Scout public, for a day at least.

Rothman and five others were arrested. In the trial that followed, the jury, seven of whom were generals, colonels, and majors, found the ramblers guilty. The trespassers were given prison sentences of two to six months for "incitement to riotous assembly."

Outraged, ten thousand walkers showed up that year at their annual rally, to protest the sentences and the continued enclosure of common land. In 1935, the numerous rambling clubs merged to form an association now known as "the Ramblers." In 1949, the National Parks and Access to the Countryside Act established a comprehensive system of linear routes over private land. In 1985, the Ramblers launched "Forbidden Britain," which was a series of new mass trespasses on enclosed land. Their goals finally gained the support of the Labour Party in 1997, and in 2000, the Countryside and Rights of Way Act was passed, which granted access to private mountains, moors, heaths, downs, and registered common lands. Scotland, in 2003, passed its own right-to-roam act, the Land Reform Act, which went a step further than England's act by granting universal access to all rural land, much like the right-to-roam systems of the Nordic countries.

———

And so we have come full circle. Land that once was open had been closed off, and it has recently begun to reopen in new ways. People are no longer going to the "new commons" to graze their cattle or to collect peat. Now they are heading out to hike and camp. Walkers became trespassers. Then trespassers became walkers. And now a new age of roaming has been born.

In 2002, on the seventieth anniversary of the Kinder Scout trespass, the 11th Duke of Devonshire, Lord Andrew Cavendish, apologized for his grandfather's "great wrong" in banning people from Kinder Scout.

"I am aware that I represent the villain . . . But over the last seventy years times have changed and it gives me enormous pleasure to welcome walkers to my estate today. The trespass was a great shaming event on my family and the sentences handed down were appalling. But out of great evil can come great good."[147]

We can see from these two dukes of Devonshire, who are separated by only a couple of generations, just how transitional the notion of property is.

CHAPTER 4

An Abbreviated Journey Across Europe

*Sooner than part from the mountains, I think I
would rather be dead . . . I may be a wage slave
on Monday, but I am a free man on Sunday.*

—Ewan MacColl, from the 1930s ballad,
"The Manchester Rambler"[148]

In Sweden, they call the right *allemansrätten*. In Finland, it's *jokamiehenoikeus*. In Britain, it's the "right to roam." These terms describe the laws and customs that grant generous roaming rights to their citizens, whether on public or private land.*

Germany allows walking through privately owned forests, unused meadows, and fallow fields.[149] In Austria, Slovenia, and the Czech Republic, people can

---

* I'd like to acknowledge the scholarship of Jerry Anderson on the English CRoW Act, John Lovett on the Scottish LRSA, and Klas Sandell for his many articles on Sweden's allemansrätten. Although this chapter relies on many resources and interviews, these scholars have made my job easy and deserve special recognition.

climb mountains, explore forests, and wander the countryside. In Finland, people can go pretty much anywhere they want, including across farmers' snow-covered fields. In Portugal, people have access to the coasts. Countries that enjoy some degree of roaming rights also include Denmark, Switzerland, Lithuania, Latvia, Estonia, and Belarus. Walkers in all of these places don't have to pay money, ask for permission, or obtain permits. While several countries, such as Spain, France, and Italy, have systems of private property like our own, Europe as a whole is far friendlier to the hiker and camper than the rest of the world.

We don't have the time to discuss all of these countries, so let's abbreviate our journey across Europe and at least visit the countrysides of England, Wales, Scotland, and Sweden—countries that have established roaming laws and customs that protect landowners, deal with conflicts of interest, and give recreational freedoms to citizens and tourists alike.

The many paths of England and Wales

The rich deep green of the British countryside, arguably the quintessence of pastoral glory, beckons the sightseer with promises of an unmatched fertility and an otherworldly lushness. There seems to be an orderly perfection to it all. It is as if the entire landscape has been sculpted for the sole purpose of pleasing the human eye—these rolling hills, these rows of crops, these dark islands of forest in seas of sunlit fields. Who could resist a ramble over the undulating hillocks of Cornwall, around the stone pillars of the Salisbury Plain, or along the rain-fed mountain lakes of Snowdonia?

Naturally, with such a countryside, one of Britain's most cherished pastimes is walking. Whether it be with a dog, to the grocery store, or to the local pub,[150] walking has literally etched itself, in the form of ancient footpaths, onto Britain's landscape. In England and Wales there are 130,000 miles of footpaths, which averages out to 2.2 miles of public trail within every square mile of land.[151] These paths were used well before roads and automobiles. They originally led to springs, churches, mills, and other towns. Today, they run almost exclusively over private land, where the public is invited to climb stiles (short stepladders used to get over fences), open kissing gates (V-shaped openings in fences that people, but not livestock, can pass through), and follow paths through herds of sheep and over fields of rye. Natural England, a public body that serves England's Department for Environment, Food & Rural Affairs, reported that there were about 2.9 billion adult visits to the natural environment in England between March 2013 and February 2014, 45 percent of which were to countryside locations. Nine out of ten people in England reported having visited the outdoors at least once in the last twelve months.[152]

The subjects of nature and the rural walk can be found within the pages of some of the most celebrated English literature. It's present in the works of Jane Austen, Thomas Hardy, and William Wordsworth, who, in "Tintern Abbey," wrote that nature was "the anchor of my purest thoughts, the nurse, / The guide, the guardian of my heart, and soul / Of all my moral being."

In England, walking is more than just a brisk power walk to tone up soft calves. It's often a method of practical transportation. On a more existential level, it may connect the walker to her land, her community, and her history.

England and Wales have many miles of footpaths you may walk on, but that you may not step off of. As beneficial as paths are, having to stay on them has been, as we can imagine, a hindrance to some walkers who come from a society that loves to walk, and from a country where 1 percent of the population owns 52 percent of the land. (Today, two-thirds of the United Kingdom's land is owned by about six thousand landowners, institutions, and the Crown.)[153]

The walking rights movement, as we saw in the last chapter, steadily gained influence over the course of the twentieth century. By 2000, the movement's power was great enough that it could help push the Countryside and Rights of Way Act (CRoW) through Parliament, giving the people of England and Wales access to mountain, moor, heath, down, and common land.[154] Americans are probably unfamiliar with *moor, heath,* and *down,* which are picturesque English words for unimproved grasslands that aren't used for agricultural purposes.

The bill opened up 3.4 million acres of privately owned English and Welsh land (somewhere between 8 and 12 percent of the countries' landmass).[155] Some of this opened-up land includes highly coveted walking grounds, such as the downs in West Yorkshire from *Wuthering Heights* and the moors of Dartmoor.[156] To be clear, this land is still privately owned, though now it's accessible to the public. Additionally, in 2009, the Marine and Coastal Access Act opened up the English coastline.[157] This coastline includes cliffs, barriers, flats, banks, dunes, and beaches, ultimately forming a 2,700-mile coastline path.[158]

While CRoW opened up lots of land, the activities that are allowed on it are quite few. These activities are limited to walking, picnicking, and sightseeing. That's it. Walkers in this newly opened terrain are not allowed to build fires, hunt, fish, camp, cycle, ride horses, swim in rivers and lakes, or forage. So paddling a canoe on a river, bathing in a lake, and playing an organized game are all prohibited, unless the landowner chooses to welcome such activities.[159] Nor can walkers travel over sports fields, golf courses, or gardens. (To the British, *garden* is similar to the American use of the word *lawn*.) In fact, no one can walk within sixty feet of a dwelling. Landowners have their own set of responsibilities. They cannot post misleading signs to exclude walkers around CRoW land, and those who violate the law are subject to fines.[160]

While CRoW mostly benefits walkers, landowners get plenty of rights, too, including the right to bar public access for twenty-eight days a year. Approval for a longer period of time can be granted for reasons relating to fire prevention, conservation, and land management. Landowners are protected from getting sued by walkers if walkers hurt themselves, whether when walking or when getting around walls, gates, and fences. Landowners are responsible only if they create intentional or reckless risks for walkers.

Landowners originally were concerned about theft, property damage, disturbance to wildlife, interference with livestock, and loss of privacy, not to mention the loss of their right to exclude. Kate Conto, who worked for the Ramblers on their CRoW campaign, said that there were many irrational concerns, too. "Children would be mowed down by combine harvesters, people would be glue sniffing in the countryside, dumping their old mattresses," said Conto in a phone interview with me. "The great unwashed would be unleashed into the countryside. But there's absolutely no evidence of any of that happening. The problems they envisaged haven't happened."

While most of landowners' concerns were reasonable, there haven't been many serious examples of walkers misusing other people's lands. Since 2005, when the CRoW Act went into effect, there has been no clear evidence of CRoW-related crime. Conflicts are rare, and studies have shown that recreational disturbance has little effect on game populations such as grouse.[161]

Before the act's passage, landowners were concerned about the potential economic consequences, such as liability suits, property damage, or walking infrastructure expenses, such as stiles and kissing gates that allow for easy passage. Landowners lobbied for compensation of $56 to $72 every year for each hectare (about 2.5 acres) that would be opened up by CRoW. The public, though, favored issuing no compensation to landowners. And because the English have nothing like the Takings Clause of our Fifth Amendment, which declares that private property cannot "be taken for public use, without just compensation," compensation wasn't necessary and wasn't, in the end, given. The government's analysis suggested that the cost to landowners would be minimal: from eight cents per hectare on seldom-visited lands to $11.39 per hectare on lands that would lose hunting income.[162]

None of the talk about compensation mattered all that much because not much changed when people won the right to roam. The moors, heaths, and downs have not been overrun by droves of glue-sniffing walkers. In fact, they haven't been overrun by walkers of any kind. Kate Conto believes that people aren't exercising their right to roam because many people aren't aware of their walking rights and because many people prefer the certainty of walking on defined paths. A lot of people simply don't know where they are allowed to walk and where they are not allowed to walk. Also, because the land was off-limits for centuries, the public is still sheepish.

"It's going to take a long time for people to understand CRoW rights," said Conto. "We've only had ten years and that's not very long in terms of a cultural shift of using land. But the principle that has been established in law—that people should have the freedom to explore wild places—is hugely important. The law as currently framed is far from perfect but we can build on what has been achieved."

The Ramblers hope to expand access in England and Wales. In addition to the moors, heaths, and downs, they hope to open up woodlands for recreation next. And the Ramblers are in discussions with other countryside users, including mountain bikers, horse riders, and campers, about expanding their access rights. In the summer of 2017, the Welsh government proposed expanding access rights to cyclists and horse riders, as well as opening up coasts, cliffs, and inland waters.[163]

Despite CRoW's many shortcomings, CRoW may

give Americans a good example of a law that upholds strong private property rights and gives the public the right to walk over specific types of land. CRoW is an example of a *partial* right to roam, far different than the Scottish and Swedish systems.

The right of responsible access in Scotland

Millions of years ago, the mountains of Scotland formed a five-thousand-mile-wide mountain chain, the remains of which are scattered from North America to Norway. Kilometer-tall glaciers, as recently as a few thousand years ago, crept over parts of Scotland, carving off chunks of the mountains and steepening the valleys into the dramatic landscape we know today. Surrounding the rugged mainland is a stormy ocean and a constellation of nearly eight hundred islands, many carpeted with thick grass that's perfect for grazing cattle and sheep. North of the cities of Glasgow and Edinburgh is one of the most sparsely inhabited regions of Europe: the Highlands, a hiker's dream of glens, Munros, and deep lochs often cloaked in cool mist. Here in Scotland we might walk an old postman's route around flocks of sheep on the Isle of Harris, sleep in a bothy (a sort of rustic shelter) in the Cairngorms, or hike up a rocky path to bag Ben Nevis, Britain's tallest peak.

Like the English, the Scottish have a sense of pride in their countryside. In "Epistle to Davie, A Brother Poet," Scottish poet Robert Burns writes,

> What tho', like commoners of air,
> We wander out, we know not where,
> But either house or hal',

Yet nature's charms, the hills and woods,
The sweeping vales, and foaming floods,
Are free alike to all.

In Scottish culture there is a Gaelic tradition of thinking of the land as an open and common place for all. An old Gaelic expression says that everyone has a right to a "tree from the wood, a fish from the river, and deer from the hills." The Scottish no longer subsist on the land this way, but the attitude behind the saying still very much exists. "I think the whole notion of a right to roam is deeply embedded in the way Scottish people feel about the countryside and the way they define themselves," said Dr. James Hunter, the first director of the Scottish Crofting Federation, which formed in the 1980s. "I believe we have an absolute right to be in the hills."[164]

Like many English and Welsh people, many Scots suffered centuries of aristocratic rule when common lands were enclosed and people were forcibly removed. In the eighteenth and nineteenth centuries, thousands of people were dispossessed of their land by large-scale sheepherders in a multicentury tragedy known as the Clearances, which has become part of the national consciousness.[165] Sometimes the evictions were scenes of tragedy. Sixteen-year-old Betsy MacKay, who had been kicked off her land, said,

> Our family was very reluctant to leave and stayed for some time, but the burning party came round and set fire to our house at both ends, reducing to ashes whatever remained within the walls. The people had to escape

for their lives, some of them losing all their clothes except what they had on their back. The people were told they could go where they liked, provided they did not encumber the land that was by rights their own. The people were driven away like dogs.[166]

The Reverend Donald MacCallum, a leader of the Highland Land League who fought to regain land that large-scale sheepherders took from locals, said, "The land is our birthright, even as the air, the light of the sun, and the water belong to us as our birthright."[167]

The Clearances happened hundreds of years ago, yet even today there are not too many people living in the Scottish countryside. Scotland is owned by just a handful of people. Half of Scotland is owned by 432 owners, and 10 percent of Scotland is owned by sixteen landowners.[168] Many of these Scottish landowners are rich absentee landowners from foreign countries. Or they're rock stars, such as Paul McCartney and Ian Anderson, the lead vocalist of Jethro Tull.[169]

Although Scotland adjoins England and Wales, and although it shares a national legislature, Scotland's roaming system is worth studying separately because it is significantly different and is among the most generous in the world.

In 1999, after a Scottish referendum, Queen Elizabeth II reestablished the Scottish Parliament for the first time since 1707. In 2003, Scotland passed the Land Reform (Scotland) Act, or LRSA, which opened up the whole Scottish countryside for all sorts of recreation. Opening up the countryside was both a practical and a symbolic act. By legally acknowledging the right to access land, it was a sort of reversal of the Clearances. Now, everyone is welcome.

While the CRoW Act opened up just a small percentage of English and Welsh land, the LRSA opened up virtually all of Scotland. It made the land available for recreation, educational activity, nature tourism (such as mountain guiding), or simply transit, whether it be to church, work, school, or another village.[170] A Scot can therefore canoe a loch, swim in a river, camp in woods, hike the highlands, and take shortcuts overland to the bus stop. She can also ride a horse, bike, sail, play a team sport, sled, paint, ice climb, and do virtually anything—day or night—while the English are limited to walking and picnicking.[171]

One key difference between CRoW and LRSA was the cost of implementing each system. The English and Welsh spent a lot of money mapping the whole country, determining precisely where all the mountains, moors, heaths, and downs were. Between mapping and implementation, this boundary-drawing approach cost England and Wales £69 million, or about $102 million. England and Wales together are about the size of Illinois. If the United States were to employ a similar mapping program over its much vaster landmass, my calculations, based strictly on landmass proportions, suggest that it could cost $6.6 billion. That's twice the annual budget of the National Park Service and enough reason for Americans to reject the very notion of the right to roam. The Scottish, on the other hand, didn't task themselves with elaborately mapping their country. Instead, they just opened up the whole country, which cost them very little. The annual cost for the Scottish government to administer the right to roam is about $10 million, which is distributed to thirty-two local authorities that employ access officers, host several local access forums every year, and pay for other recreation-related costs.[172]

The English and Welsh system took five years to get under way. Implementing the system took a while because there was a time-consuming public comment and challenge period on the maps.[173] It took a while to identify where all the mountains, moors, heaths, and downs were.

"It's way too bureaucratic," said Kate Conto of the UK Ramblers about the English CRoW Act. "Way too costly. Way too confrontational. In the end, we didn't get as much access as we reasonably expected because of the way land types were defined in order to be mapped. Judgments about whether land would become accessible or not was based on things like the presence of certain plants, the underlying geology, or the positioning of fences. I live in the South Downs. You can be walking down a path, and on one side of the path there'll be a right of public access and on the other side there won't. The average person looking wouldn't be able to tell the difference between the two areas. If we had had a free hand, we wouldn't have designed the legislation that way. If we had known then what we know now, we would probably have argued for a Scottish-type model, where you have access based on a code of practice rather than based on maps. It's much simpler to implement and easier to understand."

This code of practice that Conto refers to is the

Scottish Outdoor Access Code. The code was developed by Scottish Natural Heritage, a public body that isn't quite part of the government but is funded by and works closely with the government. In this case, the Scottish Parliament approved the Scottish Natural Heritage's code, which is a practical guide for the walking public and land managers. The rules in the code aren't exactly laws; they're principles that attempt to bring order to the system without coming across as overly restrictive.

Many of the access restrictions are spelled out in the code. A walker cannot enter a home or walk onto the yard next to a home. You also can't damage property, hunt, fish, shoot, poach game, walk dogs that are not "under proper control," or travel over the countryside in a motorized vehicle.[174] Despite these limitations, the most remarkable thing about the LRSA is how open-ended it is. One of the few rules outlined in the actual law is that anyone can do pretty much anything so long as they're behaving "responsibly." The law reads:

> A person is to be presumed to be exercising access rights responsibly if they are exercised so as not to cause unreasonable interference with any of the rights (whether access rights, rights associated with the ownership of land or any others) of any other person.

This basically means that pretty much any non-motorized activity is acceptable so long as it respects landowners, other people in the outdoors, and the environment.[175] Recognizing the profoundness of this part of the LRSA, American law scholar John Lovett said that the Scottish right of responsible access represents "a vision of human flourishing bounded by little else other than common sense and a concern for the well-being of others."[176]

Hikers in Scotland cannot walk through land where crops are growing, but, unlike the English law, the Scottish take pains to give access wherever they reasonably can. Hikers, then, are free to walk along the margins of fields, through orchards, and over hay and grass fields so long as their activity does no harm to the crops during the growing season. People can even walk over most non-synthetic sports fields and golf courses (but not putting greens) as long as their access doesn't interfere with the game.[177] Worth noting: Donald Trump's new golf course in the village of Balmedie, Scotland, is a fascinating case because it's where Trump's American (and thus exclusionary) understanding of private property clashed with the Scots' far more flexible understanding. Trump built a wall around local residents' properties and equipped his security guards with handcuffs, and his staff took humiliating photos of a sixty-two-year-old woman urinating during a walk near a beach.[178] Across Scotland, controversy, damning news editorials, local ire, and lawsuits followed.

Landowners in Scotland are prohibited from putting up signs, fences, or walls for the purpose of keeping people off land. It's even prohibited to let hedges of vegetation grow to deter walkers.[179] But of course a law like this wouldn't win the support of a country if it didn't take the interests of landowners into consideration. When I mentioned Scotland's "right to roam" to Rob Garner, who works for Scottish Natural Heritage and who was one of the principal authors of the Scottish Outdoor Access Code, Garner corrected me and said the preferred term in Scotland is the far less sexy "right of responsible access."

"'Right to roam' is very popular with journalists," Garner said. "It's a nice little encapsulation. But it doesn't convey the balance. The right to roam only conveys one of two halves. The Land Reform Act gave rights, but the Scottish Outdoor Access Code sets out what the responsibilities are." (Responsibilities such as keeping your feet off of sensitive crops or leaving bird nests undisturbed.) In other words, protecting the interests of the environment, of businesses, and of landowners was critical from the start. The law isn't just about the public's roaming privileges. It's about the public's *responsibilities*. That's why Garner said the "right of responsible access" is a better term for Scotland's new roaming regime.

Landowners have often been well looked after in the courts. In one court case, landowners Graham and Margot Tuley wanted to prohibit horse riders from entering a trail they had maintained because the horses were causing erosion and damaging the trail. After an initial ruling against the Tuleys, a higher court eventually ruled in the Tuleys' favor, and on this area of the Tuleys' property, people were thereafter allowed to walk but couldn't ride horses.[180] In a separate case involving different landowners, walkers complained about a pair of landowners who locked their gate to all walkers because a few hooligans had been littering and making noise at night. The sheriff ruled that because of the legitimate desire to keep out the young men, the gate could in fact remain locked at night, but it had to be left open for everybody else during the day.[181] Landowners can temporarily close off land for up to five days of the year (far fewer than England's twenty-eight),[182] and they may request a longer period as long as they consult with a local authority and notify the public. Landowners can close off land to spray crops with pesticides, cut down trees, move animals, or hold a festival.[183]

Not everything has been figured out, though. Landowners take issue with walkers not managing their dogs, and the public reports problems with paths blocked by signs and vegetation.[184] Simon Craufurd and his two siblings own the six-hundred-acre Craufurdland Country Estate near Kilmarnock, Scotland. Craufurd said members of the public frequently leave litter on his property, which has been owned by his family for eight hundred years. Members of the public often walk through his yard and go right up to his home to have a look. "I had the privilege of enjoying growing up here on the estate and the feelings that gave me, and I don't think there's any reason why others shouldn't be able to enjoy that same freedom, as long as they're doing it in the responsible way," said Craufurd. "We do constantly have problems with those who don't understand the details of [the law]. Whoever conjured up that phrase ['the right to roam'] should be strangled because there is no responsible access in that phrase."

Despite its imperfections, the law remains to this day very popular among the Scottish public, and complaints from landowners are few. Malcolm Combe, a legal scholar at the University of Aberdeen, said the law has been very successful. "Any time someone tries to chip away at access rights, there's always a backlash," said Combe. "I think it would be fair to say that anyone trying to repeal the new access regime would find themselves persona non grata with the Scottish public."[185]

One of the reasons why there have been so few snags with the LRSA is the use of local access forums. There are thirty-two local access forums in Scotland. These forums meet three or four times a year and are made up of about twelve members who represent interest groups, such as anglers, canoeists, farmers, landowners, and the people employed by the government to make the LRSA work. Together, these interest groups talk about and resolve issues.

Before the passage of the Scottish LRSA, in many parts of the country, people were not sure what they could and could not do. There existed (and continue to exist) public rights of way, allowing people to go from one public place to another, such as to a church or to a marketplace. But it wasn't clear that people could legally roam. Roaming was a long-established and mostly accepted custom, but without the clarity of a law, people didn't always feel at ease on other people's property. They often felt as though they were intruding or doing something illegal. With the passage of the LRSA, suddenly a hiker and mountain biker such as Dr. Katrina Brown could feel comfortable.

"It was completely different," said Brown, who studies the relationship between laws and cultural norms as a human geographer for the James Hutton

Institute. "You could just relax in a way you couldn't before because you knew you were allowed to be there. You knew that if you weren't causing harm, you were within your entitlement to be doing what you were doing."

It's not just walkers who are more comfortable. Now that the legality of an old custom has been cleared up, the government agencies that deal with public health and recreation can officially recommend getting out into the private countryside for exercise. Also, businesses—such as bed-and-breakfasts and guiding companies—can advertise recreational opportunities in the surrounding countryside.

Cycle Wild Scotland, a business that trains mountain biking guides and leads mountain bike trips, is among those businesses that have profited from the right to roam. "We have benefited from the right to roam in many ways," said Lisa Fuchs, who helps run the business. "Jules [Fincham, the top coach and guide] doesn't have to factor in the problems of trespass when going places, but in a much broader sense all strands of our business—training and assessing mountain bike instructors and guides, bike school, consultancy, and technical advisory work— have grown steadily and at a rate that doesn't look like it is going to slow down." Cycle Wild Scotland has benefited from the International Mountain Biking Association, which routinely gives Scotland high marks in its annual report card. In 2005 and 2006, the association honored Scotland with the coveted Global Superstar award, in part because of Scotland's right of responsible access.[186] "I imagine that in a time of social media," said Fuchs, "the word got out to the mountain biking community very quickly and eventually made its way to the tourist board and decision-makers."

Between 2004 and 2007, mountain biking in Scotland surged in popularity. The 7stanes district—an area that includes seven mountain biking trails in the south of Scotland—had a 120 percent increase in visits.[187] In 2009, annual income generated by mountain biking in Scotland was more than $90 million.[188] The right of responsible access has been important for a country in which tourism is a top industry. A 2010 study conducted by Scottish Natural Heritage found that nature-based tourism brought in an annual £1.4 billion (or $1.85 billion) and supported 39,000 jobs.[189]

As we've seen, estate and castle owner Simon Craufurd has legitimate complaints about litter and privacy issues. Despite these issues, he has ultimately embraced the law. On their six hundred acres, Craufurd and his siblings have opened up a mountain bike trail, a forest school, and a forest daycare area. He hosts an annual "mud run," where people cycle their bikes through the boggy parts of the estate. Next to a loch on his property, he is building a cafe, as well as "glamping" (or "glamor camping") accommodations, and high-wire walkways through the woods, which visitors will pay to walk along. (Landowners are welcome to charge for access to improved attractions, such as a high-wire walkway.) He wishes to share the estate with the public for the benefit of the local community, while using the right of responsible access—and all these new visitors—as a business opportunity. "My vision for the estate is that it becomes something that more people will use," said Craufurd. "And I'm trying to create a business model essentially that will allow my family and future generations to continue to own Craufurdland Estate." While litter and invasions of privacy remain issues for Craufurd, he has observed a notable reduction in vandalism and antisocial behavior. "Public access on the estate has had a very positive effect on reducing the number of people who come on the estate for undesirable reasons, whether it be lighting fires or getting drunk or taking drugs," said Craufurd. "Those activities have vastly decreased since we've had the increase in public access because those [vandals] are looking for somewhere where they're not going to get disturbed and where they're not going to get caught. By having lots of people on the estate, those areas become very difficult for them to find, so they find somewhere else."[190]

———

After the law was passed, outdoor recreation surged in Scotland. According to a Scottish recreation survey, the percentage of Scots who made at least one yearly visit to the outdoors for leisure and recreation rose from 67 percent in 2004 to 82 percent in 2013.[191] Fifty percent of survey respondents said they visited the outdoors on a weekly basis.[192]

There have of course been snags, one of which has been public education. The three steps for creating a system of public access in Scotland were: 1. Create a law, 2. Create an access code that spells out appropriate behavior for access takers, and 3. Educate the public about the law and access code. Katrina Brown said that steps one and two worked out just fine, but that the third could have been carried out better. It wasn't that the Scottish government failed to publicize their access code, she said; they did that well enough. The problem was that they didn't reach out to specific groups, Brown said. Take mountain bikers, who share paths with horse riders, for instance. "Lots of well-meaning mountain bikers think they should pass horses and be really quiet because they might frighten the horse," said Brown, "when actually what frightens the horse is just suddenly appearing."

The problem is that the Scottish people's relationship with the land was severed centuries ago, and many of today's urban Scots have not had a close relationship with the natural world in their lifetimes. After rural people were kicked out of the countryside, they migrated to industrial cities such as Glasgow and Edinburgh to find work. The urban population now makes up about 80 percent of the Scottish population, many of whom are not familiar with what constitutes good outdoor behavior, especially in situations that require more than just common sense, as in our case with mountain biker and horse rider collisions.[193]

"There will be a lot of people coming who don't have what other people might think is common sense," said Brown. "So the task at hand is not just having a law and a code, but to go from the code to common sense, and that's a harder thing. That's cultural. That's about practice and a million repetitions of hearing and seeing a million things."

This is a difference between Scottish and Nordic outdoor behavior, which became apparent to Brown, who is part Norwegian, on a recent trip to Norway. Outside of the town of Trondheim, Norway, she noticed a big group of teenagers with a campfire in a forest. "I thought to myself, 'Oh my God. That's just going to be such a mess in the morning,'" said Brown. "I ran past the next day and it was absolutely spotless. They completely cleaned up after themselves even though they'd been drinking and carousing and everything. I thought that that would never happen in Scotland. Maybe somewhere, but it would be very rare. I guess the question is: Can Scotland get that back? Scandinavians never became as disconnected from their country as we have, so in a way it's just easier for them. Plus, they have much, much more outdoor kindergartens, outdoor schools, forest schools. We have some of that here, but nothing on their scale. Most children in Scotland are not getting much outdoor learning. They're getting one or two outdoor trips a year, but that's not enough to make culture. If their parents are not outdoorsy, then the kids don't have much of a chance. On the litter side of things, it's still an issue here. Two persistent complaints are litter and dogs."

What can Americans learn from the Scottish LRSA? One thing is that opening up the whole country would be cheaper and easier than opening up a few specific types of terrain that require expensive and periodic mapping. American landowners may wish for more restrictive language than what is in the Scottish law, but the law's loose structure has worked for the Scots. The Scots have shown that dealing with things locally and on a case-by-case basis might be better than applying an overly specific law to a nation as geographically and demographically diverse as the United States. Another thing that Americans might learn is that Scotland's (as well as England's and Wales's) history of dispossession made people want to fight to regain lost lands and rights. We in America have many groups who have been dispossessed of their land—Native Americans, African Americans, Mexican Americans, and even white Americans. This history of dispossession, enclosure, and the growing power and land ownership of the "1 percent" could play a role in our own narrative about reclaiming lost rights.

Katrina Brown has gotten so used to Scotland's right to roam that on a recent visit to Syracuse, New York, she recalls feeling boxed in. The sense of freedom and the restorative qualities of nature are now cherished resources for her and many Scots.

"People in our research say that [nature] keeps them sane and that it's the only way they can stay on the right side of the crazy life we have. The more we lead a modern life, the more we need it."

Every man's (and woman's) right in Sweden

Sweden is a land steeped in history and ancient legends, from the steel violence of the Vikings to the golden voices of ABBA, from the Norse gods wielding war hammers to the girls bearing dragon tattoos. In the arctic Lapland, caribou snack on ripe cottongrass under the always-shining summer sun. In the winter months, Swedes snowshoe amid spruce trees clumped with snow under the waving multicolor curtains of the aurora borealis. Hikers can head south through pine and birch forests, around chilly blue lakes, along the edges of deep-green potato fields, and then between the rows of spring apple trees dripping white flower petals.

The Nordic countries (Denmark, Iceland, Norway, Sweden, and Finland) offer some of the most generous roaming rights in the world. Landowners in Denmark and Iceland have a bit more power to exclude, but Norway, Sweden, and Finland offer responsible access to virtually the whole countryside. People can take part in a wide range of activities including camping, swimming, building campfires, gathering wild produce (flowers, mushrooms, and berries), and of course hiking, so long as there is no disturbance to privacy or interference with someone's business.

We'll focus on Sweden's allemansrätten ("every man's right") because it has been studied more than the systems in the other Scandinavian countries, and because it is among the most successful, comprehensive, and longest-running roaming systems in the world.

Allemansrätten provides all the basic freedoms of the Scottish system, though gathering natural foods such as berries and mushrooms is included as well. Some of the typical areas are off-limits: cultivated farmland, military zones, and private gardens. Hikers are required to stay out of a landowner's *hemfridzon* (or "sphere of privacy"), which could mean a distance of seventy-five yards or so, but it could vary based on the house and its relation to the terrain. Some natural resources cannot be taken, such as grass, stones, peat, gravel, and trees. And fishing and hunting are separately regulated and are not a part of allemansrätten.[194] Vandals can be fined for damaging property.[195] In sum, both tourist and Swede can access most of the public and private land in Sweden as long as they're not in a motorized vehicle.

Allemansrätten is a word that has been around

for only about a hundred years, but the tradition of open access to land in Scandinavia goes back centuries. The Scandinavian landmass has always been sparsely populated, and distances between villages have always been long. To travel to faraway villages, people used the forests in between for sustenance—they ate berries, used timber to repair carriages, and gathered fallen wood to build fires. People didn't think of these forests as belonging to any one person. Rather, the forests were common lands, and the use of them was a traveler's right. Between 1350 and 1734, laws that gave landowners the right to exclude were comparable to rights that landowners have today: A landowner may exclude others only to maintain the economic value of his land and to protect his privacy.

Unlike other parts of Europe, Sweden saw far fewer rebellions and revolutions over the ownership of land. There was no feudal system either, in which only a few men controlled the lives and lands of everyone beneath them. In the seventeenth century, when the Swedish aristocracy was at its peak, the peasants owned a remarkable 40 percent of the land. (The aristocrats also owned 40 percent, and the Crown owned 20 percent.) Swedish peasants during this time were even represented in Parliament—a far cry from the debased position of British and French peasants, who were being killed or shipped abroad. Law professor Heidi Gorovitz Robertson suggests that, because all Swedes played a part in the political system, "strong property rights never became a coveted or critical need, or an issue for intense political debate and controversy." And by the time the bourgeoisie obtained power, land rights had already been well established. It was simply too late for elites to toy with property laws as they liked.[196]

Using the countryside for travel and for collecting natural resources needed for survival goes back thousands of years, but the use of the outdoors for the sole purpose of recreation began in the late nineteenth century. The modern idea for allemansrätten was born in the 1930s, when Swedes began to desire more opportunities for outdoor recreation. So, for Sweden, allemansrätten is something that is both old and new. Different generations have enjoyed access to the countryside, but for very different purposes.

Interestingly, there is no official allemansrätten law. It was, however, included in the Swedish constitution in 1994, which states: "There shall be access for all to the natural environment in accordance with the right of public access." Rather than specific legislation, there is an informal code known as the "golden rules," which form the tradition's guiding principles. These rules can be summed up with the credo, "Don't disturb. Don't destroy."[197]

Proponents of allemansrätten are reluctant to formalize the custom into law, perhaps because they fear that walking rights might get lost in a series of strict entanglements, as has happened to a certain degree under the English and Welsh CRoW Act. The Swedes are proud that allemansrätten is embedded in Swedish culture, and Swedes fear that legalizing a cultural norm may come with unforeseen consequences. Anna Sténs and Camilla Sandström write that Swedes may worry that regulating allemansrätten "would mean that everything left outside of the description would automatically belong to the private landowner."[198] In other words, a formalized law runs the risk of tarnishing the currently open-ended understanding of the custom.

Allemansrätten's legal informality has been challenged in recent years. Fruit-harvesting companies have brought in large groups of foreign workers, sometimes from Thailand, to pick berries, a practice that many Swedes believe takes advantage of the deliberately nonlitigious tradition. Yet the desire to keep allemansrätten out of the law books is so strong that even worrisome practices such as commercial berry picking have not been outlawed.

Rather than creating a broad-sounding and possibly restrictive law, keeping allemansrätten local—in both its implementation and conflict resolution—has been a key to its success. Problems, perhaps regarding a homeowner's privacy, typically are resolved before there is a need to go to the courts. New Zealand academics Richard Campion and Janet Stephenson interviewed twelve Swedish landowners about allemansrätten, and all twelve suggested that problems could be solved "through negotiated solutions and education." Many landowners acknowledged the role of regional and municipal planning authorities in negotiating solutions. Local resolution lightens the burden on the local police and courts.[199]

Like the systems in the United Kingdom, allemansrätten has its issues. The Federation of Swedish Farmers wishes for less commercial use (as in the case of large-scale berry picking). But allemansrätten, as a system and concept, is uncontroversial, well loved, and hugely popular. It's a source of national pride. The Federation of Swedish Farmers supports allemansrätten and does not desire an allemansrätten law, preferring to work things out with recreation groups.[200] One of the landowners interviewed by Campion and Stephenson said, "If the public accept farmers, then farmers should accept the public. Especially here, where we are so close to the city. It's a nice thing, it's in our roots. Actually, I don't know how to live without it."[201]

Polls show that the Swedish people cherish allemansrätten. In 2004, of the twelve thousand respondents to a FjällMistra survey, 94 percent fully or partly agreed that allemansrätten is important to defend.[202] Eighty percent of respondents said allemansrätten is important for their own recreational needs while only 42 percent said the same about Swedish nature reserves and national parks.[203] Even the people in the countryside, who are most likely to experience the negative effects of allemansrätten, agree almost unanimously (98.5 percent) that there is a need to defend allemansrätten.[204] Studies show that over 90 percent of the population hikes in a forest at least once a year.[205]

One of the reasons why the Swedes couldn't bear to lose allemansrätten is the role it plays in the Swedish economy. Sweden, especially the northern part of the country, is considered one of the last wildernesses of Europe. Tourists come from all over Europe to see it. Between domestic and international tourists, allemansrätten significantly contributes to the nature-based tourism industry, which brings in close to $1.9 billion a year in Sweden.[206] In a survey of nature tourism businesses in Sweden, 80 percent said the right of public access is a factor in their success, and 43 percent said it was of "very large importance."[207] Only 4 percent of Swedish companies considered public access an "obstacle." In 2017, Visit Sweden, the country's tourism board, launched a clever marketing initiative by putting up their whole country for free on Airbnb. (The Swedish homes and hostels aren't free on Airbnb, of course. The point is that all the meadows and lakes and mountaintops are free.) On the Visit Sweden Web page for the "freedom to roam," Visit Sweden writes, "Sweden has no Eiffel Towers. No Niagara Falls or Big Bens. Not even a little Sphinx. Sweden has something else—the freedom to roam. This is our monument."[208]

While landowners are not entirely satisfied with the public's education about the responsibilities that go along with allemansrätten, the average Swede is a pretty conscientious and knowledgeable lover of the outdoors. In a national survey, 90 percent of respondents answered questions correctly about what the public is and is not allowed to do, such as camping, mushroom foraging, timber cutting, and keeping dogs on leashes.[209]

Many Swedish schools are nature schools (*Naturskolor*), which emphasize engagement with nature and that teach ecology. As early as 1957, Sweden introduced "Skogsmulle," a mythical forest creature who was created to inspire a child's sense of wonder in nature. Culturally, Sweden embraces something called *friluftsliv*, which translates to "open air life" in English, but the translation doesn't quite capture the gist of the term, which to a Swede might combine elements of outdoor recreation, philosophy, and lifestyle, hinting at something closer to a spiritual connection and a sense of harmony with nature.[210]

Implementing allemansrätten in the United States would not be an overnight process. Allemansrätten is deeply rooted in Sweden's past of commons and peasant rights, and it has thrived under a socialist government that values equality and resource sharing. Still, there are many important lessons for Americans. Sweden's use of local authorities to mediate disputes has preserved order and satisfied all parties. The role of the Swedish Environmental Protection Agency for information is crucial. And the cultural belief in *friluftsliv* and the educational outreach to instill good outdoors behavior have fostered an environmental conscientiousness in citizens who are, for the most part, tidy campers.

———

These countries' roaming systems have their imperfections and their flaws, but they work. Because of these roaming systems, millions of people have access to natural environments. For England, Wales, Scotland, and Sweden, access to the countryside is considered a natural right—a right that Americans once had but that we have lost.

Despite our blistered feet and our sore shoulders, we have yet one more country to visit and more than a few "No Trespassing" signs to ignore. We shall head to America, the land where the people once roamed.

CHAPTER 5

The Land Americans Once Roamed

A man's health requires as many acres of meadow to his prospect as his farm does loads of muck . . . A town is saved, not more by the righteous men in it, than by the woods and swamps that surround it. A township where one primitive forest waves above, while another primitive forest rots below—such a town is fitted to raise not only corn and potatoes, but poets and philosophers for the coming ages. In such a soil grew Homer and Confucius and the rest, and out of such a wilderness comes the reformer eating locusts and wild honey.

—Henry David Thoreau, "Walking," 1862

In September 1867, a twenty-nine-year-old John Muir set off on his first big adventure. His goal was to walk from Louisville, Kentucky, to the Gulf Coast of Florida, taking the "wildest, leafiest, and least trodden way I could find."[211] Carrying a small bag and a plant press to collect specimens, Muir walked through forests, drank from streams, and slept wherever he found a place to rest his head, indoors and out. Freed from the factories of Indianapolis, where he had almost lost an eye in a machine accident, he relished the natural splendors of the American South, writing about them in his trademark effusive and reverent prose. In Kentucky, he called the entrance to Horse Cave a "noble gateway to the birthplace of springs and fountains and the dark treasuries of the mineral kingdom."[212] His walking path up the Cumberland Mountains of Tennessee was "covered up like a tunnel by overarching oaks," but every once in a while the forest opened up for a mountaintop view of the scenery below: "the most sublime and comprehensive picture that ever entered my eyes."[213] He swam across rivers and hung his clothes and paper money to dry. He walked over dunes, grasslands, sunflower groves, and railroad tracks.

Muir's journey was no leisurely stroll. In Florida, he described elbowing through a tangle of "knotted vines as remarkable for their efficient army of interlocking and lancing prickers as for their length and the number of their blossoms."[214] In a swampy forest, a man inquired whether Muir carried "shooting irons," so as to, Muir suspected, find out whether Muir would be easy to rob. Muir then reached into his pocket (grabbing nothing because nothing was there) and said, "I allow people to find out if I am armed or not."[215] When he ran out of money, he slept on a bed of moss for five nights in Bonaventure Cemetery in Savannah, Georgia, where at night he tossed into the bushes some poor frog or snake that he felt crawling on him.[216] In Florida, he was diagnosed with typhoid fever and had to put his journey on hold for three months.[217]

Muir's walk across America had all the features of a proper adventure: sublimity and hardship, encounters with generous folk and inhospitable strangers, rambles through grand scenery and impossible terrain (all of which Muir, admirably, somehow never ceased to revere). It was a one-of-a-kind journey. Muir was not one of the thousands who every year walk the California trail that bears his name, to see exactly the same sights as everyone who came before and everyone who comes after. He was the inventor of his own path, and his journey would help shape him into the remarkable man who would, later in life, lead the fight to save America's dwindling wildernesses.

One of the most interesting things about Muir's book, *A Thousand-Mile Walk to the Gulf,* is that he never mentions that he was trespassing over other people's property. There weren't any confrontations about the fences he'd hopped. There was no talk of the dangers of getting shot for trespassing. He writes of neither "No Trespassing" nor "Private Property" signs.

In 1860s America, walking over people's land did not mean what it means to us today. Americans had been hunting and fishing and walking on each other's lands since before our country was founded. People thought of land that was unimproved (which means no crops) and unenclosed (which means no fences) with a flexibility and nonchalance that many of us today would find unimaginable.

None of this is to suggest that America doesn't have private property in its roots. In 1620, the starving, disease-plagued Pilgrims of Plymouth Colony (of present-day Massachusetts) were members of a commune in which everyone shared the fruits of everyone's labor. But as the colony languished, the Pilgrims, in 1623, made their first major democratic decision when they voted to allow individuals to plant their own private plots of corn. "And so assigned to every family a parcel of land according to the proportion of their number," wrote William Bradford, the eventual governor and author of a history of the colony. "This had very good success, for it made all hands very industrious."[218] John Winthrop, an English Puritan who led the second wave of immigrants to the colony in 1630, outlined his theories on property in a pamphlet published the year before. Winthrop said that land is free to any who "possesse and improve it"—a theory that predates Locke's similar "mixing toil with land" theory by about half a century.[219] Property, in the great American experiment, was not given to people by royalty or by God; it was obtained through labor.

For the Founding Fathers, some 150 years later, private property was not a sacred institution, not an inevitable outcome of human nature, and not something handed down by God. Private property wasn't even obtained through labor. The Founders had something simpler in mind. For them, private property was *law*. That's it. Private property was acquired because governments passed laws that made land acquirable. Jefferson, let's remember, was all for letting the government meddle with land ownership. He endorsed the dividing up of large estates and the issuing of property taxes, and he even dabbled with the idea of ending land inheritance to avert an aristocracy from developing. To Benjamin Franklin, private property was a "Creature of Society, and is subject to the Calls of that Society, whenever its

Necessities shall require it."[220] Thomas Paine in *Agrarian Justice* wrote that:

> All accumulation . . . of personal property, beyond what a man's own hands produce, is derived to him by living in society; and he owes on every principle of justice, of gratitude, and of civilization, a part of that accumulation back again to society from whence the whole came.[221]

John Adams thought that the only way to preserve "the balance of power on the side of equal liberty and public virtues, is to make the acquisition of land easy to every member of society."[222] A bill James Madison introduced in Virginia gave people hunting rights on private unenclosed land.[223]

The Founders were no doubt leery of the system of land ownership in England, where the aristocracy owned most of the land. While Americans rightly cherished private property, the accumulation of massive holdings of land—despite being prevalent throughout the slave-holding South—was looked upon as a potential evil that was too reminiscent of the Old World.

A common theme that weaves through the Founders' rhetoric on property was a call for justice, equality, and the good of the community. The aims of the Founders are often misrepresented today by libertarians, who would like for us to think that the Founders and the American Revolution stood for individual rights, an unregulated economy, and small government. That could not be further from the truth. The Revolution, according to historian

Gregory Alexander, was not about liberty for individuals. It was about the liberty of citizens to work together as a self-governing community.[224] "The central dilemma of American politics," Alexander writes, "was not thought to be the protection of individual freedoms against collective encroachment, but rather, the protection of the public rights of the people against aristocratic privileges and power."[225] George Washington, after the Revolutionary War, asked for "Citizens to cultivate a spirit of subordination and obedience to Government, to entertain a brotherly affection and love for one another, for their fellow Citizens of the United States at large."[226] Things were no different decades later in Jacksonian America, where, "Freedom and regulation . . . were not viewed as antithetical but as complementary and mutually enforcing," writes historian William Novak. In early America, state governments passed laws that placed restrictions on a great many matters, including issues of contract, morality, and social life.[227] In regard to property, states passed laws that aimed to prevent the giant estates of Europe from taking root in American soil. Virginia imposed a twice-yearly tax on land holdings larger than 1,400 acres. North Carolina banned the purchase of tracts larger than 640 acres. Several colonies forced landowners to forfeit land that had gone unused for two years.[228]

Perhaps the Founders' flexible and egalitarian views on property were influenced by their own experiences roaming over private land. As a boy, John Adams roved around Braintree, Massachusetts. Biographer Page Smith said that Adams "knew by heart every pond, creek, and swamp, every fold, hill, inlet, and indentation, and venturing farther, every island within a skiff's range."[229]

Thomas Jefferson's father saw to it that Jefferson was properly acquainted with the forest. As a boy, Jefferson "stalked or rode through the southwest mountains in hot pursuit of game, or sat on the banks of streams, an expert with the rod," writes biographer Claude Bowers.[230]

On the grounds of Ferry Farm, George Washington's boyhood residence on the Rappahannock River, crowds came and went over the property to get to the ferry when the weather was nice and when court was in session.[231] In 1748, a sixteen-year-old Washington set out on a daring surveying expedition over the Blue Ridge Mountains and through the Shenandoah Valley, where he'd paddle canoes through whitewater rapids, hunt turkey, and sleep under bearskins.[232] (These territories, it should be said, were not private; they were soon-to-be-settled lands that had been taken from Native Americans.)

As a boy, Benjamin Franklin and his friends stole stones from a house builder and built a wharf in a salt marsh along the Charles River.[233] In ponds, he'd hold a string attached to a kite that drew him across the water "without the least fatigue and with the greatest pleasure imaginable." Perhaps these boyhood kiting experiences helped inspire Franklin to conduct his historic kite experiment later in life, when he and his son William ventured out into a storm in Philadelphia to capture lightning from the sky. The record isn't clear, but biographer Philip Dray writes in *Stealing God's Thunder* that the experiment probably took place on the commons or near an old private cow shed on what is now the corner of Race and Eighth Streets.[234] It may well be that Franklin and his son conducted America's most famous scientific experiment on private land while exercising their right to roam. (Speaking of famous science experiments, it should be added that when the Wright Brothers, in 1903, became the first human beings to fly, they were on private property in Kitty Hawk, North Carolina, though they did obtain permission from the landowners.)

It may be safe to assume that many of our eighteenth- and nineteenth-century leaders—in their new and sparsely populated agrarian nation—freely roamed over land, if just during their boyhoods. Ulysses S. Grant (1822–1885), the commanding general of the Union Army in the Civil War and the eighteenth president, grew up in Georgetown, Ohio. As a boy, Ulysses roamed around the newly settled Georgetown, often visiting a creek about a mile away. He fished for chubs and shiners, swam in swimming holes, and ice-skated. One time he skated for so long that he came home with frozen feet that his mother thawed out by wrapping his feet in bacon and smoking them.[235]

In the early America that our Founding Fathers and Mothers lived in, the land west of the Mississippi was an unforgiving frontier, a wilderness populated by potentially hostile Native Americans. To the east, forestland was being converted into pasture and cropland at a dizzying rate. Barbed wire had yet to be invented. Fences were few because building them was time-consuming and expensive. Most of the country was considered open range, where people let their cattle and hogs graze. There probably weren't many "No Trespassing" or "Private Property" signs, and people were allowed to hunt anywhere, sometimes even on private land enclosed by fences. In 1850, less than 10 percent of the South was enclosed, meaning that 90 percent of the South was like a giant roamable national park. Less than 1 percent of Florida and Texas was enclosed.[236]

Early Americans had a different attitude about property. Sure, they were no doubt territorial when it came to property—their homes, their possessions, their crops, their animals. But Americans then were not territorial in the way we are now when it came to people walking on their land. Unenclosed land and unimproved land was shared the same way that we harmoniously share air and sunshine today—we do it thoughtlessly and without controversy. In this way, "America was the land of liberty," writes Eric Freyfogle (whose remarkable scholarship in *On Private Property* and *The Land We Share* has informed much of this chapter).[237]

Take, for example, an 1818 case in South Carolina that centered on a landowner who tried to shoo a hunter off of his (unenclosed and unimproved) property. After what was presumably an animated and interestingly worded conversation for which posterity is sadly lacking the transcript, the hunter disobeyed, and the case made its way to the South Carolina Supreme Court. The court ruled that hunting on unenclosed and unimproved land "has never been disputed, and . . . has been universally exercised from the first settlement of the country up to the present time." The court went on to say that "the forest was regarded as a common, in which [the public] entered at pleasure." These rights were so entrenched in early American society that the court said, "a civil war would have been the consequence of an attempt . . . to enforce a restraint on this privilege."[238]

In early nineteenth-century America, the country was as roamable as one of our national parks is today. Ordinary people, though, were not using the outdoors so much for recreational hiking and camping as for sustenance, for hunting, for grazing livestock, and it's probably fair to assume, for a little bit of fun. Out in this great and seemingly endless national park, anybody who wasn't black or Native American could wander, hunt, gather wood, and even let their animals graze.

Not only could early Americans wander and hunt on each other's lands, but militias could even train on other people's lands. In 1831, a South Carolina militia cut down more than one hundred pine saplings on a landowner's property, yet the South Carolina court ruled that not only was it okay for the militia to use private property, but it was okay for the militia to cut down private trees. Four years later, the court ruled that it was okay for road builders to cut down private trees, even when the trees were on enclosed property (unless the trees were ornamental or cultivated, or unless the landowner objected in advance of the felling).[239] The public felt at such liberty to use private land that some people called for extending hunting to enclosed lands.[240] Virginia allowed people to mine for ores on unimproved private land if they came with a justice of the peace. If valuable ores were found, the prospector was allowed to mine and had to pay the landowner only for damages.[241]

The trespasser typically had the advantage in

court disputes. Without iPhones to capture footage, it was tough for landowners to prove that people had trespassed. Juries were friendly to so-called trespassers, and penalties were so light that they failed to deter future offenses.[242] Free access to land was critical for many early Americans, and any infringement on those access rights was not taken lightly. When eccentric millionaire Orrando P. Dexter bought seven thousand acres of property in the Adirondacks and closed it off to the locals who had long been using it, he was shot and killed in 1903 while driving his buggy down his impressively long driveway. It is said that even the local schoolchildren knew the murderer, but no one turned him in. Charges were never filed.[243]

Access to private property was important to Americans because it ensured that ordinary people could not be dominated by the wealthy. Open land provided economic and political independence for those who were less well off, while placing limits on the powers of rich landowners. When owners tried to control how their unenclosed land was used, they were engaging in unpopular and, to many people's eyes, plainly immoral behavior.[244]

It may seem to some readers that early Americans were lacking in some of our modern-day liberties, namely our liberty to post signs like "No Trespassing: Violators Will Be Shot, Survivors Will Be Shot Again." But the liberty of a few may be a tyranny to the many. While early American property owners *did not* have the liberty to exclude, as we currently do, American citizens *did* have the liberty to roam, as we currently don't. When both sets of liberties (the liberty to exclude vs. the liberty to roam) are weighed, the nation with a liberty to roam has, I would argue, a clear gain in overall liberty. There's no simple way to quantify liberty, but, given the fact that most Americans have little to no land, I think it's fair to say that there are many more people who stand to gain from the right to roam than there are people who stand to lose.*

A landowner may very well, and very reasonably, argue that the right to roam is an infringement of his right to exclude and his freedom to create a vast zone of privacy. We're left with a choice then: 1. To give strong powers to landowners and limit the greater public's freedoms (which is our current situation), or 2. To reduce the powers of property owners and give freedoms to the greater public.

I am in support of choice number two. There is behind any law in a democracy a question of moral legitimacy. What makes the laws that define private property morally legitimate? What makes it morally legitimate to fine a country walker for walking on someone else's land? Or what makes it morally legitimate to grant landowners the right to exclude? A better question: How shall we test whether a law is morally legitimate? I'll borrow an answer from Eric Freyfogle: "In my mind, the only persuasive justification covering land ownership is that property rules foster the common good, and with ben-

---

* Even though I've spent a paragraph discussing it, I don't believe the question of "What property system generates more liberty for the most?" is the best question we can ask to determine the moral legitimacy of a law. I'm much more comfortable asking, "What system is most just?" which I'll discuss more in Chapter 6.

efits that spread widely to essentially all citizens. When a particular element of property law fails that test—when it does not foster the common good—then it is not morally grounded." Because the right to exclude does little to serve the common good, I tend to think that it, as a law and custom, fails the moral test.*

None of this is to say that we should bring all of the early American roaming customs back. Most would agree that it's good that militias can't train in our backyards or chop down our trees. It's good that livestock are not free to wander across our railroads and interstate highways. It's good that hunting and fishing are regulated; otherwise wildlife would quickly vanish, as much of it did back in the nineteenth century. But I have described our free-roaming origins because we need to remember the freedoms we once had. We can reclaim the best of our past while leaving behind those aspects that are

---

* I anticipate the argument that an exclusionary system of property *does* serve the public good because it promotes, among other things, economic activity, which benefits the landowner and society at large. A right to roam, though, does not have to get in the way of economic activity. As we've seen in right-to-roam countries, such as Sweden, hikers are not allowed to disrupt or interfere with economic activity. On another note, let's go back to the question of moral legitimacy for a moment as it relates to the right to exclude. It should be added that there are certainly cases in which the right to exclude *can be* morally legitimate, such as with highly sensitive wildlife habitat, where wildlife would be threatened by walkers. For this reason, some public wildlife lands are off-limits, particularly during breeding seasons.

incompatible with modern times (like the free-spirited and wandering hogs).[*]

You don't have to look too hard to find prominent early Americans who embraced the right to roam. Mark Twain (1835–1910) grew up in the floodplain of the Mississippi River, a landscape of hills, caves, and the wild banks of America's great river. For weeks Twain and his friends worked to dislodge a rock the "size of an omnibus." The rock rolled down Holliday's Hill and crashed into a building.[245] Twain fished, and he foraged for pecans and berries. At night, he and his friends would roam the streets of the town of Hannibal, Missouri—around drunks sleeping with hogs, through the graveyard on the northern hill, and to the dark levee. Twain remarked later in life, "I can call back the solemn twilight and mystery of the deep woods, the earthy smells, the faint odors of the wild flowers . . . I can call it all back and make it as real as it ever was, and as blessed."[246]

Many of our great American writers, like Twain, roamed early America. Louisa May Alcott (1832–1888), the author of *Little Women*, would visit Henry

---

* It's also good to keep early American history in mind because there will likely be detractors who will use the knee-jerk argument that such and such a system dishonors the Founders and ignores the nation's heritage and traditions. I hope I've persuaded the reader that this argument would be altogether untrue. Americans have a heritage of nearly unrestricted roaming, and the Founders might very well be aghast to see that modern-day America is so closed off, so unneighborly, and, in many ways, so unfree.

David Thoreau and pass afternoons with him on a little boat on Walden Pond. Or she'd roam the hills and woods of Massachusetts.[247] "I remember," wrote Alcott, "running over the hills just at dawn one summer morning, and passing to rest in the silent woods, saw, through an arch of trees, the sun rise over river, hill, and wide green meadows as I never saw it before. Something born of the lovely hour, a happy mood, and the unfolding aspirations of a child's soul seemed to bring me very near to God."[248]

Nebraska author Willa Cather (1873–1947) rode a horse over the sparsely populated Great Plains countryside that "was mostly wild pasture and as naked as the back of your hand."[249] She said, "That shaggy grass country had gripped me with a passion I have never been able to shake."

As an adolescent, Walt Whitman (1819–1892) roamed along the edges of Long Island's Hempstead Plains, watching cow processions and listening to the "music of the tin or copper bells clanking far or near." Whitman wrote that he spent "intervals many years, all seasons, sometimes riding, sometimes boating, but generally afoot, (I was always then a good walker,) absorbing fields, shores, marine incidents, characters, the bay-men, farmers, pilots."[250]

Ernest Hemingway (1899–1961) grew up roaming in the wilds of Northern Michigan. Hemingway's father would take the young boy out to the open countryside outside of their town of Oak Park, Illinois. During summers, the family would retreat to Walloon Lake near Lake Michigan, where, in the surrounding wilderness, Hemingway honed his skills as a young fisherman, hunter, and naturalist.[251]

In a more recent example, Annie Dillard (born

1945), who has been called a modern-day Thoreau for her observations of nature in the wild spots of the Blue Ridge Mountains of Virginia, wrote about her experiences in her Pulitzer-winning *Pilgrim at Tinker Creek*. The book could be alternately titled *Trespasser at Tinker Creek* because many of her excursions were over private land. "When I slide under a barbed-wire fence, cross a field, and run over a sycamore trunk felled across the water," wrote Dillard, "I'm on a little island shaped like a tear in the middle of Tinker Creek." It was there where she'd watch "water striders patrol the surface film, crayfish hum along the silt bottom eating filth, frogs shout and glare, and shiners and small bream hide among roots from the sulky green heron's eye."[252]

Our private lands were not just used for hunting by the middle and lower classes, or as pleasure grounds for the American literary elite. They were the cold, wet, and thorny passages to freedom for thousands of runaway slaves. Slaves often began their journey by escaping into the woods and swamps near their plantations, navigating their way north by alternating between the easy passage of roads and the safer cover of the woods.

Leonard Black, a slave from south of Baltimore, escaped from his enslaver and took off for Boston. On the way, two Georgian slave traders with dogs hunted him. When Black heard them coming, he took to the woods and climbed a tree, where he stayed for nine hours as his pursuers searched for him below.[253] James Pennington, the "Fugitive Blacksmith," recounted in his memoir his daring escape from Maryland. After multiple failed attempts, he succeeded in escaping his captors by dragging himself "through briars, thorns, and running vines" and "wading marshy ground and over ditches." He ate Indian corn from harvested fields while taking cover in a shock of corn (a tepee of cornstalks assembled to dry the corn in the field), grinding the hard corn with his teeth before falling asleep.

Once these runaways found their way onto the Underground Railroad—a network of roads with stations on abolitionists' properties—their conductors often hid them in thickets, cornfields, and creek bottoms.[254] Fergus M. Bordewich, author of *Bound for Canaan,* writes of Harriet Tubman's prowess in the wild:

> Thanks to her years in lumber camps, she could find her way through the woods as skillfully as any of the old Nanticokes who had once roamed the land. When circumstances called for it, she could also slither through tall grass like a snake, flat on her stomach, using only her arms and the serpentine motion of her body to propel herself forward.[255]

Sometimes fugitive slaves didn't just travel through our private wild lands; they actually sought refuge in them. Along the Virginia–North Carolina border there is a vast forested swamp called the Great Dismal Swamp, where escaped slaves (known as maroons) formed remote settlements. They hunted, fished, gardened, and sometimes lived their whole lives in these inaccessible places, sometimes in subterranean dwellings.[256]

For these African-American men and women, the woods and creeks and swamps of private America weren't at all places to experience the joy of freedom, as they were for free men like Muir. On private land they suffered, shivered in the morning dew, and trembled as their pursuers passed by. Nevertheless, the wild places of private America were paths *to* freedom for thousands of Americans.

Many of our most prominent environmentalists got their start—and perhaps their inspiration—from their roamings over private land. John James Audubon (1785–1851), the painter and ornithologist, was a prolific traveler, taking off on a series of expeditions into the wild to find birds to draw. After visiting a neighbor's eight-foot-thick sycamore tree, which housed a village of chimney swallows, he wrote that "thousands of Swallows were flying closely above me, and three or four at a time were pitching into the hole [of the hollow branch] like bees hurrying into their hive."[257]

Theodore Roosevelt (1858–1919) was a self-made outdoorsman. Roosevelt was a sickly and asthmatic youth who remembers being roughed up by two bullies so effortlessly that they handled "me so as not to hurt me much and yet to prevent my doing any damage whatever in return."[258] To improve his physical constitution, he set off on excursions into the Adirondacks, and he later journeyed for a thousand miles through Maine's North Woods, and then its coast. He hunted game birds in Minnesota, Illinois, and Iowa, and he hunted buffalo in the Badlands of the Dakotas.

As a young man, Bob Marshall (1901–1939), one of the founding members of the Wilderness Society, was, with his brother, among the first to climb all forty-two of the Adirondacks' peaks above four thousand feet. (The Adirondacks were largely protected by the state by then, but it's likely that Marshall roamed over more than a little private land on these excursions.) Later, he headed to Alaska to be among the first white men to explore the Brooks Range north of the Arctic Circle.

Aldo Leopold (1887–1948), the author of *A Sand County Almanac*, spent his youth hunting, hiking, and observing. The young Leopold had a fascination with birds, and he'd go with a friend to nearby ravines—like Bonn's Hollow and Ransom's Hollow outside of his native Burlington, Iowa. He'd walk into the woods or take a skiff along the edges of the Mississippi.[259] Later, at prep school in Lawrenceville, New Jersey, his biographer Curt Meine writes, Leopold was off on daily tramps in the winter countryside. "Within a month he had acquainted himself with the area for ten miles around, drawn a map, and applied his own labels . . . He typically set aside an hour or two each day, more if his schedule allowed, and took off with a small notebook and his grandmother's opera glasses."[260]

Rachel Carson (1907–1964), author of *Silent Spring,* would seek solitude in the hills and creeks that fed into the Allegheny River near her home in Pennsylvania.[261] Later, as a student, she'd walk along the Massachusetts shore, "looking in the tide pools, finding new organisms among the rocks or clinging to the seaweed . . . captivated by the sounds, smells, and rhythm of the ocean," writes her biographer Linda Lear.[262]

Henry David Thoreau's (1817–1862) saunterings, though far less ambitious than Muir's adventurings, provide another prime example of the carefree walking spirit of nineteenth-century America. Thoreau was never one to turn down a good walk. He walked to pick berries, to study the habits of bullfrogs, to enjoy the moonlight, and to idly ramble over his town's surrounding countryside. "I think that I cannot preserve my health and spirits," Thoreau wrote in his essay "Walking," "unless I spend four hours a day at least—and it is commonly more than that—sauntering through the woods and over the hills and fields, absolutely free from all worldly engagements."

Thoreau wrote that Concord "affords many good walks," so many that, despite walking almost every day for many years, he claimed to have "not yet exhausted them." "I can easily walk ten, fifteen, twenty, any number of miles, commencing at my own door without going by any house, without crossing a road except where the fox and the mink do: first along by the river, and then the brook, and then the meadow and the woodside."

Thoreau's essay "Walking" serves as both an ecstatic paean to the country's free-roaming past and a grim forewarning of what was to come. "Possibly the day will come," Thoreau wrote, "when [land] will be partitioned off . . . in which a few will take a narrow and exclusive pleasure only—when fences shall be multiplied, and man-traps and other engines invented to confine men to the public road . . . Let us improve our opportunities, then, before the evil days come."[263]

He was right. The evil days came. Over the next 150 years, America would be shut down.

The right to exclude

Let's start in the South. After the Civil War, with the end of slavery, cotton growers faced a major labor shortage, so states passed laws to starve the newly freed blacks into submission.[264] It was made illegal for blacks to graze hogs in common areas, to hunt, or to collect food. "If black people could feed themselves, even partly, from wild food, they could negotiate for better pay and working conditions," said property scholar Brian Sawers. "Closing off the outdoors was an important part of a program of legal aggression, aimed at strengthening the bargaining power of white landowners and returning blacks to as near a condition to slavery as possible." These initiatives were carried out almost immediately. When the Louisiana legislature met in 1865 after the war, they passed a resolution that acknowledged the end of the war and that criminalized trespassing.[265]

There were other, less racial, more economic forces that ended Americans' right to roam. It became less expensive to fence in livestock on the previously open ranges, so suddenly much more of the country was enclosed. With technology, enhanced farming techniques, and a diversified economy, ordinary people were no longer hunting and gathering as much as they used to—so there was no longer an impassioned group of proponents who had a serious stake in maintaining their roaming rights. Railroad companies wanted to close the range to reduce costly cattle accidents, and farmers argued for closing the range to livestock (and consequently people) so that farmers wouldn't have to put up fences around their crops.

After the Civil War, state legislatures began changing the laws governing hunting. Plus, there was a new spirit of free enterprise taking hold in post–Civil War America. Property law was changing to accommodate industry, which demanded the freedom to create noise, pollution, and erect tall buildings that would often block light and air. An 1873 ruling by the New York Supreme Court shows how the rights of property owners began to trump the needs of the greater community: "We must have factories, machinery, dams, canals and railroads. They are demanded by the manifold wants of mankind, and lay at the basis of all our civilization."[266]

There also were changes in how law was being practiced. "Many courts became hostile toward the work of legislatures and regulators," writes Eric Freyfogle. "They viewed new statutes with suspicion. And they increasingly allowed landowners to use their property rights as a shield to resist new laws they disliked."[267]

In 1922, the US Supreme Court in *McKee v. Gratz* ruled that in areas where there is a "common understanding," the public is permitted to hunt, fish, and travel over private land. However, this right is revoked the second the landowner posts a "No Trespassing" sign or builds a fence. This is referred to as a landowner's "right to exclude," which, over the years, has grown more powerful and absolute in a series of Supreme Court decisions.

It is unclear when the first "No Trespassing" sign was posted. In the early days, it's safe to assume that they were homemade, and they probably weren't mass manufactured until the twentieth century. Searching the Library of Congress's digitized newspapers, which contain issues from 1789 to 1924, we learn that the first mention of a "No Trespassing" sign—in newspapers at least—was in 1880 in *The Cecil Whig*, a newspaper in Elkton, Maryland. In a piece of satire, the author recommends keeping a "sharp lookout for the familiar sign, 'No Trespassing Allowed!' That's the place to look for game and that's why the notice is put up." We can deduce from the word *familiar* that the sign had some life before the article. For the next fifty years, these newspaper articles show that the sign, for the most part, was a butt of jokes. It was called "rude" and "crude," and was even used to foment antiwar sentiment. In 1914, in a little rhyme called "No Trespassing," Arthur B. Baker wrote,

> Oh Mother Earth! Oh Mother Earth! They've gone and fenced your face, excluding many members of the so-called human race; and there the toads may hop and spring, the little brooks may flow, the busy birds may fight and sing, but children cannot go. Behind the fence a millionaire may venture once a year, to breathe a cubic foot of air and shoot his private deer. But when the band begins to play "My Country, 'Tis of Thee" and Uncle Sam essays to make a soldier out of me, and send me forth to perforate the lusty foreign lout, I can't forget the sign that says: "No Trespassing: Keep Out!" I lack enthusiasm for my country's proud defense, so largely is it hid away behind a selfish fence.[268]

The closing down of America was just getting started. In the 1905 Connecticut Supreme Court case *Graham v. Walker,* residents of Connecticut wanted access to a property owner's land because his land contained a historic footpath that connected Lisbon to the nearby town of Taftville. In England, requests such as these have been successful, but the Connecticut Supreme Court ruled that the roaming rights the English enjoy just don't apply in America.[269]

Other cases such as *Kaiser Aetna v. United States* (1979) and *Loretto v. Teleprompter Manhattan CATV Corp.* (1982) have strengthened the right to exclude. In *Kaiser Aetna v. United States,* the Supreme Court said that the right to exclude was "one of the most essential sticks in the bundle of rights that are commonly characterized as property."*[270] The case is significant because the Court's opinion, says property law scholar Brian Sawers, "spawned a whole jurisprudence of exclusion." In other words, the ruling strengthened the right to exclude to the point that it goes pretty much unquestioned today. It's considered "the core element of property." Even though expanding public access has always been the historic right of the states, states are now hesitant to expand access because the *Kaiser Aetna* ruling makes them worry that any new laws would be declared unconstitutional.[271]

In *Loretto v. Teleprompter Manhattan CATV Corp.,* the Supreme Court said that in American legal

---

* Although the Supreme Court called the right to exclude "one of the most essential" rights, the Court is merely doing so to describe the property laws of most states as a generalization. In other words, the "essential" comments were not part of the ruling, and there's no Supreme Court ruling that acknowledges the constitutionality of a right to exclude. This will be discussed more in the "takings" section in Chapter 8.

culture, landowners must be compensated for harmless intrusions, or even helpful improvements, when a landowner is kept from using even a small part of what she owns. The case dealt with a cable company that, in the end, had to abide by the Takings Clause and compensate landowners for installing wires and cable boxes on people's properties.[272] The Court's devotion to the Takings Clause makes it hard for states to create legislation to open up private land for roaming. Consider recent rails-to-trails initiatives, in which abandoned railroad tracks are converted to trails for public use. Even though a walker is less of a nuisance than a train, and even though the path has historically been a public passageway, the courts recognize that under legal precedent and the Fifth Amendment, landowners may have the right to exclude and to be compensated.[273]

America, land of the free, has been shut down one statute, one court ruling, and one "No Trespassing" sign at a time. The land where fugitive slaves made their way to freedom, where Muir's character was shaped, where the Wright Brothers conquered the impossibility of flight, where Franklin stole lightning from the sky, where writers, environmentalists, and leaders found inspiration, and where millions of early Americans got their daily dose of nature—this land has been, for the last 150 years, systematically closed off. This closing off was a boon for the minority of land-rich property owners, but it was a huge setback for the greater American community.

While it may seem that the rich, the radical

ranchers, and the big landowners are gaining power and taking over, we can also point to new patterns in property law—namely in the environmental regulations of the 1970s—that suggest that the community has actually been winning rights from big landowners. And while the public-access movement can only be described as "emerging," there are many people who find something fundamentally wrong with the fact that landowners can cut off access to beaches, forests, and fields at whim. We can point to many local organizations fighting to open up access to land and coastlines that are important to the public. In Montana, the Public Land/Water Access Association is fighting to gain access to private land so that people can cross through it to access public land. The Trust for Public Land is campaigning to safeguard our public lands from private hands. The Surfrider Foundation believes that everyone should be able to use all of America's beaches, and in 2017 the foundation launched more than fifteen campaigns in ten states to enhance and protect beach access.[274] Small groups everywhere form locally and congregate on Facebook to fight for their own favorite piece of earth, groups such as Save Ontario Ridge Trail in Avila Beach, California, or the Friends of NE 130th Beach group in Seattle, which successfully fought for access to the Pacific shoreline.

With so many Americans upset about the loss of their favorite escapes, with growing resentment of the "1 percent," and with the ridicule heaped on the radical ranchers who seized and occupied public land, perhaps Americans are ready for a change.

CHAPTER 6

Why We Need the Right to Roam

If I were to name the three most precious resources of life, I should say books, friends, and nature; and the greatest of these, at least the most constant and always at hand, is nature. Nature we have always with us, an inexhaustible storehouse of that which moves the heart, appeals to the mind, and fires the imagination—health to the body, a stimulus to the intellect, and joy to the soul. To the scientist Nature is a storehouse of facts, laws, processes; to the artist she is a storehouse of pictures; to the poet she is a storehouse of images, fancies, a source of inspiration; to the moralist she is a storehouse of precepts and parables; to all she may be a source of knowledge and joy.

—John Burroughs,
"The Art of Seeing Things"

I am drawn to the right to roam largely because of my own roaming experiences. I have hitchhiked more than ten thousand miles across North America. And I have canoed and walked thousands of miles across North America. These were journeys that led me into the hearts and homes of hundreds of complete strangers. On my hitchhikes, I got in cars and trucks driven by teachers, carpenters, oil-men, alcoholics, recovering addicts, ex-cons, house moms, carnies, Mexican immigrants, Native Americans, African Americans, and military vets. On my hike across the Great Plains, all along the way ranchers gave me water, farmers gave me food, churches gave me shelter, and cops gave me well wishes.

At the start of these journeys, I'd be scared and anxious. I knew I was putting myself in vulnerable situations with strangers. But I found that, after a while, these anxieties and fears would dissipate. Perhaps it's less dangerous for a white guy like myself, but I can say, from my experiences at least, that most people aren't out to get you. After such a journey, you learn that the American people are not nearly as scary and dangerous as our news stories would have us believe. You come to realize that Americans generally are hospitable, friendly, and kind. Once this realization sets in, you begin to move through the world in a lighter, more carefree way. You feel more trusting, more relaxed, more free.

These were some of the most liberating moments of my life, not because my adventure made me feel free. I felt free, rather, because I was operating with a new state of mind. I could trust complete strangers. And I felt free because I no longer shouldered that heavy load of paranoia. There's a relationship between trusting people and feeling free. More than getting out of debt, quitting a job, or going on an adventure, letting your guard down and just trusting may be the ultimate act of liberation. Trust is good for societies. But trust is also, I'd like to argue, fundamentally necessary for the full flourishing of a human life. Without it, we operate in a world that never truly feels like home. Without it, we're weighed down by chronic worry. A trusting state of mind is like living in a world where there aren't any "No Trespassing" signs.

Trust and hospitality can be easily found in America, but it seems like we're doing everything we can to bury the best of our society. We Americans might like to ask ourselves: What do we gain as a society from our rigid understanding of private property? What does it do to our collective psyche to hoard our lands and see our countryside littered with "No Trespassing" signs? What does the closing of America say about us as a people?

When I see unnecessary fences and rude signs, I see the worst of America: selfishness, meanness, isolation, reclusiveness, inequality, injustice, the privileges of the rich, and the sad state of our communities. An unneeded "No Trespassing" sign aggrieves me in the same way that an oil spill, a racial epithet, or bullying does.

In a "No Trespassing" culture, there's a disavowal of society, a self-expulsion from one's greater community. When I walked across parts of Oklahoma, nearly every home had a fence around it and a snarling cur under the porch. There were countless signs reading "Beware of Dog," "Private Property," and "No Trespassing." I assumed that it was just as unlikely for a neighbor to knock on one of these front doors as it was for a stranger. We live in cultural poverty when we put up boundaries. How can there be any sense of community when neighbors don't visit with one another? How can we understand the world when we're secluded and holed up? When our homes are closed off to the outside world, so are our minds. This is the poverty of not having a community, of not sharing in our country's lands and resources and collective fate. When we set ourselves apart, we become Charles Foster Kane, building up and enclosing ourselves behind the walls of our personal Xanadus. We become Montgomery Burns, releasing the hounds on visitors because we're insular, untrusting, and scared.

When we no longer identify as an interdependent part of our greater community but rather as a lord of a manor who can wall himself off from the concerns of his fellow countrymen, we are not far from sociopathy. Perhaps he begins to think it's okay to close off swimming holes and cemeteries. Perhaps he begins to wish to steal public land for his personal use. Perhaps, eventually, he does not bat an eye at polluting the portion of the stream that winds its way onward through the lives of his neighbors. When we close off America, we're losing something far more precious than our recreation rights.

Our "No Trespassing" culture is a symptom of a deeper sickness afflicting our country. The right to roam and all the civic values it represents—equality, shared resources, social trust—may be one step toward a cure.

Rebuilding social trust

In his encyclical *Laudato Si'*, Pope Francis in 2015 called for protection of "common areas, visual landmarks, and urban landscapes which increase our sense of belonging, of rootedness, of 'feeling at home.'" According to Pope Francis, our urban and rural landscapes should "form a whole" that is a "coherent and meaningful framework" for our lives. In these inviting, inclusive, and well-planned places, he wrote, "Others will then no longer be seen as strangers, but as part of a 'we' which all of us are working to create."[275]

Pope Francis is calling for fixing our deficit in trust, for making our communities feel more like home, and for making strangers into friends, acquaintances, or just recognizable faces. We don't necessarily get that from a country in which we drive everywhere. According to the Safe Routes to School organization, the number of children walking or biking to school dropped from 50 percent in 1969 to 13 percent in 2009.[276] Staying indoors, interacting with the same succession of people, and exploring video game worlds rather than the real world may contribute to the rising prevalence of fear and mistrust of people.

According to a General Social Survey of adults conducted between 1972 and 1974, 46 percent of adult Americans believed that "most people can be trusted." By 2012, only 33 percent felt that way. In a Monitoring the Future survey of twelfth-graders between 1972 and 1974, 32 percent of the twelfth-graders thought that most people can be trusted. By 2012, only 18 percent of twelfth-graders believed that most people can be trusted.[277] The fact that only 18 percent of eighteen-year-olds today are trusting suggests that there is a serious deficit in social capital and an unreasonable level of paranoia. Americans are bombarded daily with news of violent crime, though the crime rate has been falling for years. Rates of rape, robbery, aggravated assault, burglary, larceny, and vehicle theft have all plummeted since the highs of the eighties and nineties.[278] We are two times less likely to experience violent crime than in the early nineties.[279] The 2014 murder rate was 4.5 deaths per 100,000 people—the lowest rate ever recorded in the United States since data started to be collected in the 1960s. Crime, then, is not the sole reason Americans are so mistrustful. We mistrust because of much larger forces—growth of inequality, decay of social capital, loss of social trust, news organizations' fetish for stories of violent crime. These factors tend to make us believe that crime, and humanity, is worse than it is.

Might the right to roam enhance public trust and make the country more neighborly? Elinor Ostrom won the Nobel Prize in 2009 for her work studying how societies that keep a commons flourish. "There's a five-letter word I would like to repeat and repeat and repeat: Trust," said Ostrom in her Nobel Prize lecture.[280] In *Trust: A Very Short Introduction,* author Katherine Hawley sums up Ostrom's factors that enhance public trust: "a long-term situation, the opportunity to learn about others' reputations, and the possibility of communication between all the relevant parties."[281] Along these lines, agrarian philosopher Wendell Berry said, "A proper community is a commonwealth: a place, a resource, an economy. It answers the needs, practical as well as social and spiritual, of its members—among them the need to need one another." Jane Jacobs in *The Death and Life of Great American Cities* writes that for a city to maintain order there must be "an intricacy of sidewalk use . . . a constant succession of eyes." Currently in America, we have neither Ostrom's commons, nor

Berry's community, nor Jacobs's succession of eyes. What we have is social and civic decline, as described in Robert Putnam's *Bowling Alone*. No longer are we hanging out in bowling leagues and book clubs as much as we are sitting at home by ourselves watching Netflix on our tablets or listening to political talk radio in our cars.

Not only are we alone more but America's various demographic groups may be on a whole more segregated now than they've ever been. Our schools are more segregated by race than they were in the late 1960s.[282] According to Richelle Winkler, a demographer at Michigan Technological University, retirement communities segregate the old from the young to the point that we are segregated by age similar to the extent that Hispanics are segregated from whites.[283] There is income segregation, too. Subdivisions contain houses of the same style, size, and price range, which separate us from other groups by often minute gradations of income.[284]

Being separated from people outside of one's own age, race, and income level may have huge social consequences. Who today feels a sense of national unity, of teamwork, or of neighborliness with their fellow countrymen and women? Who trusts strangers anymore?

The authors of *Suburban Nation* suggest that social segregation keeps Americans from developing a sense of empathy for people from other walks of life and fails to prepare us for living in a diverse society. "The more homogenous and 'safe' the environment," the authors write, "the less understanding there is of all that is different, and the less concern for the world beyond the subdivision walls."[285]

Might segregating ourselves from people who

are different contribute to political polarization? Borrowing data from a Pew Research Center survey on contemporary partisanship, *The New York Times* reported in a 2016 article that:[286]

- "For the first time since at least 1992, the majority of Democrats and Republicans say they view the opposing party 'very unfavorably' . . . [A]round half of the members of either party said their opponents stirred feelings of fear and anger in them."

- "Today . . . 91 percent of Republicans view the Democratic Party unfavorably, with 58 percent holding 'very unfavorable' attitudes toward it. Among Democrats, 86 percent view the Republican Party unfavorably, while 55 percent hold it in a very unfavorable light."

- "The Republican Party strikes fear in the hearts of 55 percent of Democrats surveyed, Pew found. Among Republicans, 49 percent felt the same way about the Democratic Party."

- "Roughly one in three members of each party said they considered their political counterparts to be less intelligent than other Americans."

- "Exactly half of Republicans and 46 percent of Democrats said they find talking politics with a member of the opposing party to be 'stressful and frustrating.'"

There are many factors behind our incivility, and it would be absurd to suggest that the right to roam is a panacea for all of our nation's ills. But might it help? Might sharing land, seeing more people face to face, and interacting with other demographic groups help us build a sense of community with our fellow citizens?

Behavioral scientists Nicholas Epley and Juliana Schroeder conducted an experiment in 2011 in a Chicago commuter train. The researchers asked one group of participants to keep to themselves (as we normally do on trains), and the researchers asked the other group of participants to strike up a conversation when a stranger, who wasn't part of the experiment, sat beside them on the train. Most participants thought beforehand that they would be happier if they were left on their own to play games on their phone or to quietly listen to music through their earbuds, and they expected that fewer than half of the strangers they started conversations with would actually want to talk with them. The researchers found that not only did all of the strangers engage in conversation with the participants but also that the participants who were told to have a conversation reported having a more positive commuting experience than the group playing games on their phones by themselves. In another experiment, Dr. Gillian M. Sandstrom, then a PhD student at the University of British Columbia, asked participants to keep track of their social interactions with people with whom they had strong and weak ties. Sandstrom found that the participants with more interactions felt happier regardless of whether they were introverted or extroverted and regardless of whether each interaction was with a strong or weak tie. As *The New York Times* sums up these studies: "Even the bit players in our lives may influence our well-being."[287]

According to a Swedish study, children and parents who live in an area with good outdoor access have twice as many friends as people who do not. Richard Louv said that "green space fosters social interaction and thereby promotes social support."[288] In cross-national surveys, the countries with the best public trust are routinely Nordic. According to the Organisation for Economic Co-operation and Development's 2015 *How's Life?* report, Denmark, Sweden, Finland, Iceland, and Norway all scored the highest in social trust.[289] Has the right to roam played a role in enhancing public trust and social capital in these countries, which happen to be among the most roamable in the world? Many factors impact public trust (economic equality being one of the central factors), and walking on other people's lands is probably not near the top of the list. Yet, roaming is closely related to the values that make these countries so trusting: shared resources, a common natural heritage, trust in people to act responsibly, and acceptance for all of society.

The physical and mental health benefits of roaming

The closing of America's "first frontier," according to Frederick Jackson Turner in his 1893 essay "The Significance of the Frontier in American History," occurred when the American West was officially settled and the wars with Native Americans ended. Then began, according to Richard Louv in his 2005 book *Last Child in the Woods*, America's "second frontier," when agrarian livelihoods connected most of the American population to the land.[290]

This second frontier ended, according to Louv, in 1993, when the US Census Bureau decided to cease its annual survey of farm residents. The Census Bureau no longer deemed the statistics relevant. There just weren't enough people working on farms anymore. (In 1890, 40 percent of US households were in farming country, but that had dropped to 1.9 percent by 1990.)

America, today, has a largely urban population. Eighty-one percent of us live in urban and suburban environments,[291] and 60 percent of us live in large metropolises of two hundred thousand people or more.[292] Few of us grow up with close connections to the land, and fewer young Americans are playing outside. According to a study by Sandra Hofferth at the University of Maryland, from 1997 to 2003 there was a 50 percent decline in the proportion of children between the ages of nine and twelve engaging in activities such as fishing, walking, gardening, and hiking. Hofferth found that children spent nine fewer hours a week playing outside. Rhonda L. Clements, a professor of education at Manhattanville College, found in a survey of eight hundred mothers that 71 percent of mothers remembered playing outdoors every day as a child, yet only 26 percent said that their kids play outdoors every day. Interestingly, Clements also found that responses from mothers didn't change when it came to raising their kids in urban or rural environments. Clements wrote that because rural lands are restricted (or "unroamable"), rural lands do not present more outdoor opportunities for kids than urban environments.[293]

Louv's *Last Child in the Woods* popularized the term "nature-deficit disorder" and called attention to the fact that modern kids are not spending enough time in nature. In an era of overmedication, the clinical-sounding designation was controversial, but justified. The more we live our lives indoors, the less we walk, hike, and roam. Instead, we sit. Dr. Emma Wilmot of the University of Leicester analyzed eighteen studies that looked at the habits of eight hundred thousand participants. She found that inactive adults who sit for most of the day, compared with active adults, have a 147 percent higher risk of heart attack or stroke, a 112 percent higher risk of diabetes, and a 59 percent higher risk of premature death.[294]

Hippocrates, the Greek physician regarded as the father of Western medicine, once said that "walking is man's best medicine."[295] Countless studies have backed up his simple claim. In 2009, two scientists from University College London did a meta-analysis of eighteen studies on walking that involved 460,000 people who were observed for more than eleven years. The analysis found that walking reduced cardiovascular events by 31 percent and the chance of dying during the period of the survey by 32 percent. The analysis found that moderate walking—just two miles per hour and a mere five and a half miles a week—was all that was needed to get the benefits of the walking lifestyle.[296]

No one disputes that walking is good for your physical health, but we're learning more and more about what immersion in green spaces can do for our mental health. In two studies published in 2015, Stanford graduate student Gregory Bratmana found that volunteers who were directed to walk through a green section of the Stanford campus had less anxiety, better memory, and experienced less "morbid rumination" than the volunteers who walked alongside heavy traffic in Palo Alto.[297] In a similar study, conducted by the University of Essex's Centre for Environment and Society, researchers had participants walk through an indoor shopping center and through a country park with woods, grasses, and lakes. Richard Louv in *Vitamin N* sums it up best: "After the green outdoor walk, 92 percent of participants felt less depressed; 86 percent less tense; 81 percent less angry; 80 percent less fatigued; 79 percent less confused; and 56 percent more vigorous." After the indoor walk, depression increased for 22 percent of the participants and stayed at the same levels for 33 percent.[298]

In Japan, there is a practice called *Shinrin-yoku,* or "forest bathing," which is essentially walking in the woods. Physiological anthropologist Yoshifumi Miyazaki examined six hundred subjects who had taken either an urban or a forest walk. He found that the forest walks contributed to "a 12.4 percent decrease in the stress hormone cortisol, a 7 percent decrease in sympathetic nerve activity, a 1.4 percent decrease in blood pressure, and a 5.8 percent decrease in heart rate." His colleague, Qing Li, an immunologist, found that forest bathing increases our NK cells, which fight tumors and infections. Li examined Japanese businessmen who had walked in the forest. These businessmen had as much as a 40 percent increase in these life-saving NK cells. Forests, Li said, are "like a miracle drug."[299] Research also has shown that walking and green spaces can lessen the symptoms of ADHD, can enhance memory, and can spark creativity.

The American medical community might have reason to be happy about improved opportunities for outdoor recreation. Scotland, as we've seen, has opened up their countryside for recreation, and many Scottish doctors have begun to embrace something called "green care," also known as "green prescribing." Instead of prescribing pills, doctors prescribe outdoor activity for health problems that can be improved by increased physical activity. A Scottish Natural Heritage study showed that about 75 percent of green prescriptions prescribed increased walking, conservation activities, or "green gym" activities.[300] Physical activity, in treating type 2 diabetes, is not only a cheaper prescription than pills; it's also more effective. A 2002 study found that exercise and diet changes can prevent one out of seven cases of type 2 diabetes. Metformin, a pill used in diabetes treatment, prevents one out of fourteen.

Right now in Scotland, doctors' green prescriptions usually lead patients onto Scotland's "core paths" system. In the LRSA legislation (described in Chapter 4), local authorities were tasked with creating easily accessible paths for walkers, cyclists, and horse riders. Dr. Katrina Brown of the James Hutton Institute expects green prescribing to expand beyond the core paths system into the wilder countryside as the right to roam and green prescriptions become more popular.

We're already seeing the countryside used for green prescriptions in Sweden, where they've had the right to roam for centuries. Nils Hallberg, one of two people working exclusively for Sweden's right to roam within the Swedish Environmental Protection Agency, said that green prescriptions are becoming increasingly common and that the presence of easily accessible spaces in nature is a key factor in the increase. "It can be a good alternative or a good alternative in combination with ordinary medical care," said Hallberg. "For people who are depressed, a doctor will tell them, 'You should walk in a forest at least three times a week.' Since we have [the right to roam], it's easy to start prescribing fresh air to people. There are not many Swedes who have no access whatsoever to the outdoors. That's a key factor for doctors to prescribe outdoor activities."

Physical inactivity, worldwide, caused 5.3 million deaths in 2008, according to a study published in *The Lancet.* In the United Kingdom, physical inactivity causes 10.5 percent of coronary heart disease cases, 18.7 percent of colon cancer, 17.9 percent of breast cancer, 13 percent of type 2 diabetes, and 16.9 percent of "all-cause mortality."[301]

Poor health is not only a major cause of human misery; it's also a drain on a nation's economy. The American Diabetes Association in 2012 estimated that diabetes cost $245 billion ($176 billion in direct medical costs and $69 billion in reduced productivity).[302] In 2012, the Integrated Benefits Institute estimated that poor health costs the United States $576 billion annually.[303] According to the Centers for Disease Control and Prevention, inactive adults, per capita, require $1,437 more in health care costs annually than active adults. Collectively, the costs related to physical inactivity come out to be around $131 billion.[304]

Making recreation space without breaking the bank

In August 2016, one day before the National Park Service's one-hundredth birthday, President Obama announced the designation of a new national monument called Katahdin Woods and Waters, made up of 87,500 acres of forestland, mountains, and the East Branch of the Penobscot River in north-central Maine. People in the top levels of the Park Service believe the new monument is ideal for national park designation.* That would be the same path to becoming a national park that led to park status for Acadia National Park, Maine's only national park, which also was first protected as a monument. Turning a national monument into a national park should be quite simple. All that's needed is an act of Congress. But getting Katahdin Woods protected, whether as a monument or park, has been anything but simple.

Roxanne Quimby, the co-founder of Burt's Bees, made Katahdin Woods her life's work for more than twenty years. Securing the land cost Quimby $74 million. (She'd later give a $40 million endowment to the new monument.) Hundreds of thousands of dollars were spent on a Washington lobbying firm and a public relations agency.[305] Quimby funded economic studies and engaged in many rounds of public outreach to gain the support of resistant locals, one of whom told *The Washington Post*, "What in blazes are they trying to monumentalize? There's nothing extraordinary about it, except for a lot of black flies."[306] Maine's residents, the timber industry, and politicians opposed her plan, including Maine's governor. Once Quimby and her son realized that

---

* The main difference between monuments and parks is that the president can designate a monument without congressional approval. Also, monuments tend to be much smaller.

they could not get the support of Congress to turn Katahdin Woods into a national park, they began lobbying President Obama, who had the authority to create a national monument. Finally, after twenty years and more than $100 million, Quimby's efforts paid off. And yet it's still not a national park. All this trouble for a tiny national monument (one-eleventh the size of Rhode Island) in a relatively uninhabited region of the United States.

Creating a national park is never easy. It took J. D. Rockefeller three decades to surmount local opposition to create a national park in the Teton Range of Wyoming. Because of the unavailability of relatively unpopulated land, the days of big new parks are long gone. Theresa Pierno, the president and chief executive of the National Parks Conservation Association, said in an interview with *The Washington Post* that Katahdin Woods "may be one of the last, large national parks that we see in our lifetime."

If there aren't many more places to designate as national parks, then we might look to our favorite right-to-roam countries for inspiration on how they've created recreation lands cheaply and in a way that hasn't disturbed landowners.

Sweden's allemansrätten shows that a country can open up pretty much all of its territory to recreation for very little money. Sweden provides generous recreational access to about 80 to 90 percent of its landmass.* Americans are mostly limited to

---

* This is a rough estimate by Klas Sandell, a professor of human geography at Karlstad University in Sweden, whose calculation factors in off-limits developed areas, agricultural lands, and conservation zones.

roaming our state- and federal-owned lands (lands considered "public"). The public lands in Sweden, including its national parks, take up 13 percent of Swedish landmass,[307] but Swedes are legally allowed to roam over a much larger territory—again, 80 to 90 percent of Sweden's landmass.

Allemansrätten is not free, but it's also not expensive. There are two full-time workers who deal with allemansrätten for the Swedish Environmental Protection Agency. There also are a number of people on the regional and municipal level who have some allemansrätten-related duties but who aren't exclusively working with public-access rights. There are minor costs for roadside pull-offs and trash bins at popular destinations. And there is an ongoing public outreach campaign to educate the public to get out and walk, clean up litter, and enjoy the outdoors responsibly. These costs are impossible to sum up because allemansrätten is so well integrated into Sweden's economy and government. But it's also fair to say that allemansrätten is not a huge expense for the Swedish government.

Let's look a little more at the cost of protecting land in America. In addition to the National Park Service's $3 billion annual budget, there are about $12 billion worth of backlogged and much-needed repairs that have not been undertaken because of an impressive influx of recent visitors and a Congress reluctant to allocate taxpayer funds.[308] As expensive as our parks are, they're underfunded and understaffed, and there simply isn't enough infrastructure to service the more than three hundred million annual visitors. (I write this from experience, as a seasonal park ranger at the Gates of the Arctic

National Park in Alaska, where I was one of two full-time backcountry rangers who monitored the park's 8.5 million acres—a landmass equal to Maryland.) In 1904, the year the NPS started counting visitors, national parks were visited 120,000 times. In 2016, there were 331 million visits, which broke the 2015 record of 307 million visits.[309] Many parks have been flooded with visitors. Yellowstone, for example, averaged about three million visitors between 1990 and 2008. That number has steadily increased to 4.2 million in 2016.*

We can see from the increasing number of American national park visitors that the country is hankering for recreation and access to natural scenery. As amazing as our national parks are, many of them fail to provide this. We drive to national parks to "get away," but we often end up in congested traffic that is just as bad as city traffic. Yosemite National Park warns its visitors that they may be stuck in traffic for one to two hours.[310] Great Smoky Mountains National Park got 11.3 million visits in 2016.[311] During Memorial Day weekend in 2015, Arches National

---

* Outdoor recreation is also growing. According to the Outdoor Foundation, 49 percent of Americans participated in an outdoor activity between 2006 and 2015. While this participation rate has stayed about the same during that time span, the *number* of participants has increased because of population growth, from 134.4 million participants in 2006 to 142.4 million in 2015, for a total of 11.7 billion outdoor outings. The five most popular outdoor activities for adults are running, fishing, hiking, cycling, and camping. The number of hiking outings increased 25 percent between 2006 and 2015 from 30 million to 37 million.[312]

Park had to shut down because of miles of traffic. The superintendent of Arches and Canyonlands national parks, Kate Cannon, pushed to charge higher fees at peak hours. She proposed installing an unprecedented reservation system to manage the deluge of visitors.[313] In an interview with NPR, Joan Anzelmo, a retired park superintendent and a spokesperson with the Coalition to Protect America's National Parks, said, "We're running out of room for people to have these wonderful experiences."[314]

Anyone who has lived near a national park knows that natural beauty does not end at the park boundary. Around Zion National Park, which I lived next to for a few months, there is stunning scenery—just as spectacular as inside the park—on adjacent private and Bureau of Land Management land. If land was opened up not just around national parks but everywhere in the United States, many Americans wouldn't have to drive for days to get to beautiful scenery. And if the United States embraced allemansrätten, and people more readily had access to nature nearby, then visitation to our faraway national parks might drop to more manageable levels, and our natural experiences might not be degraded by congested trails and bumper-to-bumper traffic.

One might argue that newly opened private land could get overrun with visitors the same way that many of our parks are overrun, especially if this land is beautiful or near a city. This is a reasonable concern, especially in forests and farmland near heavily populated cities. Around such areas, Sweden has created "nature reserves," a designation that doesn't really have an analog in the United States. A

Swedish nature reserve is like a national park combined with private land. The landowner still has
ownership of the land, but the government—
national, regional, or local—will manage the "reserve." They'll provide toilets, walkways, and picnic
tables to protect the landowner's land from overuse
and damage. The landowner still has the right to
use the land for timber and agriculture, and if the
reserve does end up limiting the landowner's op-
tions, then authorities will provide compensation.[315]
Trails on private land in Sweden also have helped
reduce damage to the land by keeping hikers on the
trails. There are more than four hundred national
and regional trails managed by state and recreational groups[316] in Sweden, as well as four thousand
nature reserves.[317]

In the United States, one could make the case
that creating more public lands could solve our recreational crisis. But nonprofit foundations and federal and state governments have learned that
converting private property to public property is
neither easy nor cheap. For instance, the Prairie
Plains Resource Institute, a nonprofit environmental organization in Aurora, Nebraska, had to raise
$1.9 million to buy a 650-acre ranch with the hope
of creating recreation space and animal habitat.[318]
The American Prairie Reserve, a Montana nonprofit
that aims to create the largest wildlife reserve in the
lower forty-eight states, has been buying private
land and leasing public land since 2004. The Prairie
Reserve's goal is to amass three million acres.[319] As
of the fall of 2016, they had made twenty-five trans-
actions, buying 86,586 acres of private land and
leasing 266,518 acres of public land. Since 2002,

these acquisitions, as well as the cost of running their organization, have cost $34 million. The Appalachian Trail (AT) is a 2,190-mile footpath stretching from Georgia to Maine. The trail is managed by the National Park Service and the Appalachian Trail Conservancy. It was conceived in 1921, and it began as a mixture of public and private land. Private land always threatened the continuity of the trail, so in 1978 the various organizations in charge launched a land acquisition campaign that is still ongoing. (The trail and its thousand-foot buffer corridor were officially secured in 2014, amounting to 250,000 acres.)[320] This was a long, tedious, and expensive process. It involved obtaining 3,700 small tracts of land,[321] and Brian King at the Appalachian Trail Conservancy estimates that the full cost has been more than $200 million. Managing the trail requires an annual budget of $8.2 million.

Despite being loved and increasingly visited, our national parks are not havens of wildness, liberty, and solitude that can easily satisfy our roaming needs. These are not places where we can feel that we've escaped the workaday world of traffic jams, rules, and red tape. Anything but. From the moment we enter a park, we are reminded that our national parks are not wide open ranges where you can finally be free; rather, our parks are tightly controlled, overrun with people, and expensive. A seven-day pass for Yellowstone costs $30 for a car, plus at least another $15 a night for a campsite. If you decide to visit the adjacent Grand Teton National Park, that's another $30 entrance fee, plus $24 a night for a campsite.[322] And let's not forget the expense of driving hundreds or thousands of miles to get to the park in the first place.

When you are charged an arm and a leg, when you have to provide IDs, fill out permits, and submit to backcountry orientations—all in a stifling bureaucratic atmosphere—one's wilderness experience isn't very wild anymore. It's a far cry from John Muir's sense of complete freedom in the Sierras, or Edward Abbey's sublime visits to the Arches before these places were made into national parks.

William C. Leitch, writing about bureaucratic trends in the National Park Service, described his dystopian vision of our future park experience in a 1978 essay. Leitch imagined a park service, in the year 2078, that has assumed control over everything. Backpackers must apply to hike three years in advance. They must wear, along with the animals, transmitting devices so they can be monitored by the park to ensure safety.[323]

Jack Turner, in *The Abstract Wild*, said we've normalized a truly abnormal wilderness experience: "Looking at photographs of arches or pictographs, reading a guide book, examining maps, receiving instructions on where to go, where to camp, what to expect, how to act—and being watched over the entire time by a cadre of rangers—is now the normal mode of experience. Most people know no other."[324]

Not only do our national parks require long drives from home and cost an unreasonable admission, but visitors in many parks, such as Arches or Rocky Mountain National Park, are encouraged to stick to trails and camp in designated campgrounds. Many of our parks don't provide opportunities for whimsical, adventurous roaming. This is not a criticism of park policy; these rules exist for good reasons. Such rules limit erosion, protect endangered animals and plants, and reduce the damage made by too many visitors. Our national parks contain many endangered animals and some of our most spectacular natural scenery. They must be treated with special care. The parks are justified in encumbering visitors with rules and regulations, as well as charging desperately needed fees. Only the wildest, most remote, and least-visited national parks, such as Gates of the Arctic in northern Alaska, can serve as places where we may freely roam without feeling fettered by rules and fees.

Our existing national parks, and even an expanded NPS system, simply are not the answer to our future recreation needs. Between 1990 and 2013, the NPS added 3,515,278 acres of parkland (about the size of Connecticut).[325] This is an admirable addition in parkland, but it's only a drop in the bucket for a country that contains 2.4 billion acres of land and a population that has increased by about 67 million people in that time. Despite a slight gain in park service land, our federal public lands as a whole have actually declined because of heavy losses in Bureau of Land Management land, which lost close to 25 million acres between 1990 and 2013. Between the four federal agencies that manage public recreational lands—Forest Service, National Park Service, Fish and Wildlife Service, and BLM—our net loss was more than 17 million acres between 1990 and 2013.

So despite a growing population and increased demands for recreational opportunities, the public is not gaining more recreation spaces. And we're losing private recreation spaces, too. Projections show that suburban and exurban areas (exurbs are often prosperous commuter communities beyond the suburbs) will increase 15 to 20 percent between 2000 and 2050, and that cropland and forests will decline 4 to 7 percent during that same period.[326]

The current distribution of our public lands doesn't help things, either, since these public lands are unevenly distributed across the country. Federal and state governments own 806 million acres of land in the United States.* These public lands make up 35 percent of America. The fact that over one-third of our land is publicly owned may mislead us into thinking that we have more than enough public land to satisfy all of our recreation needs. But a closer look shows that most of this land is inaccessible to most Americans. Most of this public land is concentrated in low-population western states. (Alaska alone has 329 million acres of public land, which is 41 percent of all public land in the United States.) The five states with the highest percentages of public land—Alaska, Nevada, Utah, Idaho, and Wyoming—have 62 percent of the public land in the United States but only 3.7 percent of the US population.[327] The far more populous states on the East Coast—say, the original thirteen colonies plus Washington, DC—have 30 percent of the US population but only 3.2 percent of the public land. Many major cities, like Chicago, have very little public land within a hundred miles of the city.

Lack of public walking space isn't just an East Coast problem. Several Midwestern and Great Plains

---

* I'm not including the 14 million acres of Department of Defense lands that are generally inaccessible to the public. The state numbers come from a 1995 estimate by the National Wilderness Institute.

states are almost entirely owned by private landowners. States with very little public land (less than 3 percent) include: Illinois, Indiana, Nebraska, Oklahoma, Ohio, Texas, Iowa, and Kansas.

Since we're discussing America's roamable lands, we shouldn't leave out trust land in the United States, which amounts to more than 8 million acres, 72 percent of which are accessible to the public, according to the Land Trust Alliance's 2015 census report.[328] That adds another 5.8 million acres of roamable land in the United States, or .25 percent of all US land. Trust lands do well to protect particularly sensitive ecological areas, and in some cases serve the public's recreation needs. But these places are too small, too few, and too expensive to play a serious role in meeting our recreation needs.

Aside from being out of reach for most Americans, our public lands are, in many cases, inaccessible or off-limits. These facts bear repeating: 9 percent of BLM lands are inaccessible because they're barricaded in by private property, according to a 2004 report to the House Appropriations Committee. This means that 23 million acres of *public* BLM land cannot be reached by the public because of private landowners. In 1987, it was estimated that to purchase easements for restricted public lands it would cost $96 million.[329] That we need to pay landowners nearly $100 million to get to our own land is, to put it nicely, absurd. The Forest Service does not have reliable numbers, and Forest Service officials from western states, speaking under the condition of anonymity, say that millions of acres of Forest Service land are inaccessible as well, partly because points of public access have been bought and closed off by private landowners. Of the 566 Fish and Wildlife refuges, 104 of them, or 18 percent, are off-limits because of resource protection, public safety, or staff shortages.[330] Many of the acres of state-owned land that I included in the above public land calculation are neither natural land nor accessible. Of these 197 million acres of state-owned land, only 18 million acres, or 9 percent, classify as state parks and recreation areas, among a few other designations, according to a 2015 report from the National Association of State Park Directors.[331] On paper, 35 percent of America is public and thus presumably roamable. But in reality, the percentage of lands that we are allowed to walk on and that we have reasonable access to is a far less impressive number.

Let's sum up the trends: Park Service visitors are coming to increasingly congested national parks in record numbers. We're not gaining more public spaces. Many of our public lands are off-limits to us. We're steadily losing farm and forest spaces, and unless we install a network of bullet trains, most of our public green places will always be out of reach. And finally, the US Census Bureau shows that we can expect our population to grow by almost 100 million people to 417 million by 2060.[332] What we have in the making is a crisis in recreation.

Let's also consider America's world-class, but ultimately inadequate, trail system. Unlike Europe's smaller historic trails, which serve the communal purpose of connecting towns to towns, and towns to agricultural places, America doesn't have a heritage of ancient trails, especially after we displaced or outright destroyed the Native American tribes, along with their legacies and trails. America, rather, has long "thru-hiking" trails, such as the Pacific Crest, Continental Divide, and Appalachian Trails. These trails range from about 2,100 to 3,100 miles in length. These long hiking trails, unlike Europe's shorter historic trails, aren't so much necessary and practical footpaths as bold inventions created by eccentric visionaries, like Benton MacKaye, or committees of trail makers, like the Pacific Crest Trail System Conference.

We compensated for our lack of local walking paths—paths that appeared naturally because they were needed—and worked around our problem of private property by putting together these great north-to-south trails, which have no practical, utilitarian purpose and can't be easily reached by many people. Only the most adventurous backpackers or day-hikers who have cars can make use of these trails. These long trails are not for the European *community*; they're for the American *individual*. They pass through undeveloped and fairly wild land: perfect ground on which the hiker can test her mettle, depend on herself, and become the self-reliant citizen that our country so values. Yet, as bold and beautiful as these trails are, they do little to give the casual walker a quiet path where she can get her daily dose of nature.

Because of our scarcity of historic paths, because few of our villages ever had a commons, and because of our vehicle-dependent lifestyles, America is compelled to create, rather than eliminate, property lines when establishing recreation spaces. We have seen how costly it is to acquire land and rearrange property lines for parks. If America wants to provide more opportunities for recreation, then we need to think differently about our property lines. Our property lines ought to be less rigid and more flexible, less closed and more porous, less barbed wire and more friendly stile.

Sustainable development

Not only is acquiring trails and parks expensive but historically the acquisition of private land has often involved the expulsion of the land's inhabitants, usually Native Americans and poor white farmers.[333] The conservation movement, though no doubt well intentioned, has its own dark past. To set aside land, we have destroyed livelihoods and expelled people from grand, natural places such as Yellowstone, the Adirondacks, and the Grand Canyon. In what is now Yosemite National Park, soldiers pushed out the Ahwahneechee, a local tribe that for a while returned to perform entertainment shows for visitors. The tribe eventually was evicted. Their homes were burned in a fire-fighting drill in 1969.[334]

Sweden's allemansrätten, on the other hand, is friendly to landowners, industry, and private property because, by opening up private land, no one has to be removed. Landowners are free to carry on their work. Instead of creating conflicts of interest with landowners, allemansrätten has actually *improved* relations between rural landowners and the urban public who come out to experience other people's lands. This is because allemansrätten provides an opportunity for education, interaction, and mutual understanding. "People working with forestry and agriculture think the urban people don't understand what they are doing," said Klas Sandell, a professor of human geography at Karlstad University in Sweden. "There's a rift between urban people and rural people. So, from a landowner's perspective who's working the land, the right of public access makes the urban people more involved and helps them understand what it is to live in the countryside, what it is to work with forestry, agriculture, food, timber, energy. I had a talk with a farmer and he says that's the main benefit of the right to public access: It makes people roaming around in-use landscapes understand what we are doing, how we are doing it, and why we are doing it. If you're walking through a wilderness corridor, you won't understand anything about what it is to be a farmer in the United States."

This is certainly true for most Americans. In American national park lands and on our national scenic trails, we walk through planned wildernesses that hardly represent America as it is. The Appalachian Trail, for instance, does everything it can to avoid cities and industry. It goes through only a few horse and cattle pastures, as well as a handful of towns. Few Americans have any idea what life is like for New York dairy farmers, Iowa corn farmers, and Wyoming ranchers. We barely get to see industrial zones, land that's fracked for oil or gas, or the factory farms where chickens, pigs, and cattle live and die by the billions. Our parks and trails intentionally conceal the realities of the American industrial and agricultural economy, keeping walkers in a thin and protected corridor of wilderness on a continent that is becoming increasingly less wild. Our industrial zones are segregated from our recreational zones, and because we aren't exposed to the ugly parts, we can't care as much as we should about how these places are being used. They are out of sight and out of mind.

Sweden's allemansrätten, on the other hand, allows hikers to have outdoor experiences on land that's developed, whether for industry or agriculture. These city people who roam rural lands have exposed themselves to lands used for timber, farming, and energy extraction. This, according to Professor Sandell, leads the urban public to urge lawmakers to develop the countryside sustainably. "It is very important that people have contact with the landscape that is used so they can develop a linkage," said Sandell. "Urban people can develop a linkage to a landscape that is used for human purposes, where people are producing food, creating energy, and taking care of the waste."

———

How we protect nature tells us "as much about ourselves as about the things we label with [nature]," writes William Cronon.[335] What does our protection of national parks say about us? Let's first consider what a national park is. By and large, our parks are places that attempt to capture not only a pre-European North America (five hundred years ago) but an America without any people (about thirteen thousand years ago). These parks are for the most part purposefully devoid of permanent human communities. They are reproductions of wildernesses that attempt to represent a pristine, Edenic nature that strangely has no people. And because a *reproduction* cannot completely reproduce what exactly was there before, national parks are actually *reinterpretations* of wilderness. These reinterpretations are largely determined by the political climate, by the desires of Park Service management, and most of all, by the public's prevailing notions of wilderness.

We cherish these reinterpreted wildernesses. Edward Abbey said that our parks are "holy places" and "sanctums of our culture" that should be given the same deference that we give to our cathedrals, our museums, and our legislative assemblies. Surveys from Pew Research Center and Cornell University's Roper Center show that the public's satisfaction with national parks has been consistently strong, ranging from 77 to 85 percent in the 1980s and 1990s. And even though many Americans currently have an extreme distrust of and dislike for the federal government, the national parks are one of the few government-run programs that the public consistently supports, giving 74 percent and 73 percent satisfaction ratings from participants in Pew and Gallup polls in 2015.[336]

Cronon argues that thinking of our national parks as special zones of conservation and environmental protection affects how we treat the rest of America. Let's consider the Great Smoky Mountains National Park, the most visited national park in America. The park straddles the North Carolina and Tennessee border and contains an especially picturesque chain of Appalachian peaks. The Smokies, known for the clouds of foggy mist that blanket the landscape, are now known for a new kind of smoky fog. The Smokies have some of the worst air quality in the entire national park system. Shockingly high levels of air pollutants have obstructed visibility so badly that visitors can expect to see from mountaintop overlooks no farther than twenty-five miles (compared to ninety-three miles in clean air). Visibility has dropped 80 percent from levels reported in airport records in 1948.[337] On particularly hazy days, visibility is reduced to less than a mile in air that is "as acidic as vinegar," according to the park's air quality report. It becomes so hazardous that the elderly and children are urged not to hike in such conditions. Ozone pollution, created when nitrogen oxides mix with hydrocarbons in sunlight, has had a devastating effect on the living environment. Thirty species of plants show leaf damage, including 90 percent of black cherry trees and milkweed plants. At the highest elevations, ozone pollution is twice as bad as readings taken at nearby commercial centers in Knoxville and Atlanta. To make matters worse, pollutants in the air stick to things, and the park has the most sulfur and nitrogen deposits of all monitored national parks. These deposits limit the availability of calcium, which harms vegetation and stream life, and it pollutes the water.

What do all these problems have in common? They've all originated outside, not inside, the park's borders. Power plants, automobiles, and factories in nearby cities produce heavy doses of nitrogen oxides. Ozone pollutants ride the air currents, travel to the Smokies, and become trapped in the mountains. These very serious environmental issues seem so staggering because they're present in a protected wilderness that ought to be an example of natural purity. Environmental issues such as these, most people would think, should be found only in industrial centers. But pollution doesn't confine itself to city limits, just as wild animals do not respect the borders of national parks.

William Cronon argues that environmentalists, proud of what we've preserved, tend to lose sight of what happens outside the borders of these protected zones. Celebrating our national parks the way we do may encourage us to engage in something called "moral licensing." Taking special care of one section of land gives us the moral license to do whatever we want with the rest of America, as we've done with the industrial centers around the Smokies, the fracking regions of Pennsylvania, the nitrate-rich Iowa groundwater, the Love Canals, and the 1,336 Superfund[338] sites spread across the country. In other words, patting ourselves on the back for setting aside the Katahdin Woods allows us to destroy America's less dramatic landscapes—our sacrifice zones.

In his widely cited essay, "The Trouble with Wilderness," Cronon appreciates our national parks, but he argues that often we idealize a distant wilderness while forgetting to appreciate the "environment in which we actually live."[339] Protecting large tracts of land is not necessarily a bad thing, he said, but because there's knowledge of "protected areas" in the collective consciousness, it then becomes justifiable to permit rampant industrialization at home. Author Michael Lewis, summing up Cronon's message, said, "[W]ilderness preservation is not a reaction against industrialization, but actually enables the process. Wilderness is the cultural sleight of hand that makes (often grotesque) contemporary development and exploitation mentally acceptable."[340]

Cronon said that this understanding of wilderness represents an "escape from responsibility." It's an "illusion that [enables us to] wipe clean the slate of our past and return to the tabula rasa that supposedly existed before we began to leave our marks." By mistakenly separating civilization (which is unnatural and unclean) and wilderness (which is beautiful and immaculate), we "leave ourselves little hope of discovering what an ethical, sustainable, honorable human place in nature might actually look like." The failure to recognize a middle ground that embraces the wildness in our farms, private forests, and suburban lawns (while only thinking of places like parklands as "wild") may be one of the reasons why there aren't strong enough restrictions on urban-generated pollutants.

Cronon claims that our idealization of wilderness is fundamentally false because it rests on a foundation of invented history: "There is nothing natural about the concept of wilderness. It is entirely a creation of the culture that holds it dear, a product of the very history it seeks to deny." Because our wildernesses are devoid of the peoples who have inhabited them for millennia, our parks are inherently false reproductions. They are fabricated wildernesses; idealizations that reflect not true wilderness but "our own unexamined longings and desires."

Wildness, however, is real. And it's everywhere. It's the weeds in the cracks of Atlanta's sidewalks and the air above Knoxville's city streets. And if all these little wildnesses were appreciated as much as the Smokies, the pollutants that originate in urban centers would diminish. Thoreau's oft-disputed line, "In Wildness is the preservation of the World" supports Cronon's central message. In valuing the always-real wildness over the fundamentally fake wilderness, we can embrace an honorable and sustainable relationship with our environment.

Cronon, echoing the central message of Aldo Leopold's "Land Ethic," said, "People should always be conscious that they are part of the natural world" because we are "inextricably tied to the ecological systems that sustain their lives." Cronon sounds as though he'd be a fan of allemansrätten, which has encouraged Swedes to consider the environmental value not just of a few protected pockets of wilderness but of all of their country, from its moose and grizzly habitats to its farms, fisheries, and managed forests.

Cronon suggests that *wildness* can be appreciated anywhere, but that *wilderness* is "likely to reinforce environmentally irresponsible behavior." Cronon is by no means suggesting that we get rid of wilderness areas such as Great Smoky Mountains National Park, but only that we should modify our understanding of them. Great Smoky Mountains National Park should not be perceived as one of a few cherished zones of wildness, because true wildness is everywhere.

Justice

In this chapter I've listed a few reasons why we'd be better off with the right to roam. It's not merely that we would benefit from improved physical health, mental health, and social trust. It's not merely that it would give us affordable recreation space and help us appreciate the nature all around us. All that is not enough. Those are reasons why the right to roam is merely *good*. Let me take a moment to explain why I think that the right to roam is *just*.

One could say that the prevailing philosophy of the present day is utilitarianism. This line of thinking—developed by Jeremy Bentham, John Stuart Mill, and others two hundred years ago—argues that an action is justifiable when that action creates the greatest good for the greatest number of people. In other words, to a utilitarian, an action is justifiable if it benefits 9,999 people but ends up hurting one. Utilitarianism is not without merit or lacking in examples of how it has worked well for majorities. But it has not necessarily been good for people of color in America. Slavery was once rationalized for the economic wealth it generated and the material benefits that it provided for a great many, while of course causing harm to the slaves themselves. Capitalism, to pick another obvious example, has generated enormous wealth for society, but it has often made the poor poorer.

Modern philosopher John Rawls in *A Theory of Justice* argues for a system that is fair for everyone (especially for that ten-thousandth person). Rawls calls this principle "justice as fairness." To illustrate his philosophy, he proposes a thought experiment invoking what he calls the "original position." In the original position, a group of participants is asked to come up with a set of economic and social structures for a hypothetical society that they will live in. But each participant goes into this discussion not knowing who he or she will be in this society. No one knows whether they will be a man or a woman, black or white, gay or straight, healthy or unhealthy, rich or poor, and so on. We can imagine that the sort of society that they would agree on, under such conditions, will more than likely be fair, and therefore just, for all.

Let's add in the idea of property now: Each participant may turn out to have lots of property, or none. If we were in a room with such a group of people deciding what kind of society we wanted to live in, with no knowledge of how advantaged or disadvantaged we as individuals would be, what would we decide would be the fairest system of property? Would we choose a situation like ours, where, according to the most recent numbers, the richest 5 percent own 75 percent of private land? Where the top half of 1 percent of the biggest landowners own 40 percent of the land?[341] Where many African-American landowners were pushed off their lands after the Civil War by whites? Where Native Americans had their treaties broken, their families killed, and their lands stolen? (Between 1887 and 1934, ninety million acres of Native American land fell into the hands of the US government.)[342] Where two million Americans are homeless, yet there are seven million second homes? Where billionaire John Malone jokes about a "land-buying disease" that he got from Ted Turner, each of whom owns lands larger than some states? Where the rest of us are confined to tiny lots?[343] Where minority groups are more heavily concentrated in hazardous pollution centers that increase the risk of cancer and disease?[344] Where white and wealthier communities have better access to parks, open spaces, and coastlines? Where children go without adequate and accessible green space and suffer from all sorts of physical and mental health issues?

With basic fairness, justice, and equality in mind, I think that it would be hard for anyone to claim that our current system of private property is ideal. Let's think for a moment about this accepted norm: If one person owns ten acres of land, then he, under almost all circumstances, has the right to ban *seven billion people* from those ten acres of earth. Not only does this person possess the wealth necessary to own the land, not only can he build just about anything he wants on it, not only can he plant whatever crops or graze whatever animals he pleases, not only can he get to exclusively hunt and fish on it, and not only can he create wealth and reap rising land values for himself, but he can exclude everyone else from all of the land's benefits. If ten acres doesn't sound like a big deal, then let's call it one hundred, one thousand, ten thousand, one hundred thousand, or one million acres. This man gets to close off all of this land and keep out anyone, to the point that the land doesn't really exist to the rest of humanity. No one but this one man will get to walk over that rolling hillside and view the sunset that falls behind his stand of woods. He may be charitable and tolerate others on his land, yet the American landowner still has the awesome legal power to close off his land to others the moment he pleases. Apart from a handful of environmental regulations, he can do pretty much whatever he pleases with his land, regardless of his land's complicated ecosystem, before he passes it on to his children for their sole enjoyment.

Our culture and ethics and laws would have us believe that we are the creators of our own lives, makers of our own destinies. We believe that through our hard work and our natural talents we've earned the right to possess and manage land of our own.

But we fail to appreciate how our place in the world—our health, our socioeconomic status, our life expectancy—has far more to do with when we were born, who we were born to, and if we were fortunate enough to have been swept to prosperous shores by the grand tides of history. The work of Harvard researcher Raj Chetty and his team at the Equality of Opportunity Project shows that we are only partly in control of our fates. Our likelihood of achieving economic success is influenced by factors such as residential segregation, income inequality, social capital, school quality, the year we are born, and whether we have one parent or two, among other factors.[345] Someone born in San Jose, California, for instance, has a much better chance at climbing the economic ladder than a person born in Atlanta, Georgia. Author Gregory Clark in *The Son Also Rises* has shown that our income mobility is partly determined by our surname and how our families fared hundreds of years ago.[346] If we owe our success in large part to good fortune, then doesn't it in some way delegitimize our absolute claim to the lands we've bought or inherited? We are a democracy that at least pretends to embrace equal opportunity for all of its citizens, yet those who are on top have gotten there in part because they have benefited from head starts, inheritances, and high-functioning institutions that not everyone has access to. Why, then, should someone who has disproportionately benefited from our laws and institutions have disproportionate access and privileges to the country's lands?

The right to roam, when you think about it, is actually pretty modest. Arguably, the right to roam doesn't go far enough in addressing injustices in how our society divides its resources. The right to roam is, at best, a small consolation prize for a society afflicted with gross inequality.

What I wish for is not simply the right to go wherever we please. It's more about the grander values that the right to roam represents. It's more about living in a country that values the good of the community over private privilege; a country that shares its natural resources and sceneries; a country that is trusting, neighborly, welcoming, supportive, united; a country whose people are bound to their lands and waters, and whose fates are shared. What I'm calling for, I'd like to think, transcends modern political attitudes of conservative and liberal, Republican and Democrat, because the freedom to walk in the woods is something far more timeless, far more ancient, far more fundamental to leading a good life as a human being.

CHAPTER 7

The Arguments Against Roaming

Yeah, I don't want random people walking across my property . . . Much like communism, it looks nice on paper, but in practice I don't see it ever working in America.

—Christian Taylor, *New York Times* website comment, 2016

In April 2016, I wrote an article for *The New York Times* called "This Is Our Country. Let's Walk It." The book you're reading is an extension of the article, and the purpose of each is the same: to advocate for an American right to roam. My article received several hundred comments on the *Times'* website and Facebook page. A great many comments were in support of my idea, but of far more interest to me were those from folks who had objections. I catalogued all "anti-roaming" comments. Because there are no surveys, studies, or research on the right to roam in America, these comments have been, for me, an indispensable resource. They fall into six categories:

- Thirty people (41 percent of detractors) think that Americans are destructive, irresponsible litterbugs.

- Twelve people (16 percent) expressed concern about landowners getting sued by hikers.

- Ten people (14 percent) think that all the guns in America would pose a threat to the right to roam.

- Nine people (12 percent) said that we should stick to getting our recreation on public land, or that we should just create more public land.

- Eight people (11 percent) wanted to keep their private land to themselves.

- Four people (5 percent) said the laws of Europe do not apply to the United States.

Americans are destructive, irresponsible litterbugs

It would be nice to open our land to all, but the reality of maintaining private land is more complicated. Having forty-five acres of field and mixed forest, connected to our son's larger acreage, one would assume that letting all come to walk, snowshoe, cross-country ski, hunt, and more would provide no problems for the landowner. Wrong. It is not everyone but when we had our land opened, we were picking up other people's trash, cigarette butts (fire hazard). People tromped off trail and destroyed trilliums

*and animal nesting sites. Additionally, there was
no respect for quiet hours. People would be driving
their loud snowmobiles and four-wheelers
around our trails at midnight or much later.
Hunters, who should know better, were firing
their guns inside the safety zone. People would
carve things in trees, pull off low tree branches,
and be careless in the wetlands. We gave up.
Even among cries of "It's not everyone!" the truth
is it was enough people to be considered the norm
rather than the exception. We don't pay the land
taxes for others to destroy the land, habitats, and
the peace. Sorry if that seems selfish.*

—Vicki

This argument is one we can all sympathize with.
No one wants to see litter. No one wants to pick up
someone else's trash. And no one wants to feel dis-
respected when we find other people's litter on our
property. It's a nuisance, and it can even be, as Vicki
writes, a fire hazard. But, as legitimate as this argument is, I'd like to argue that there are ways we can
educate litterers, foster better outdoor behavior, and
make life easier for landowners.

Let's consider how a set of landowner protections
would protect Vicki's land. Let's apply, say, Scotland's
right of responsible access law and see how things
might improve. For one, destroying flowers and nesting sites, as well as disrespecting privacy, would all
be considered behavior that is not in compliance
with "responsible access," which is required of all
roamers. The bad behavior that Vicki has seen or
heard would be, under this Scottish law, punishable
by fines. It's probably safe to argue, though, that a

lot of people would get away with irresponsible activity in a remote backwoods location. But, still, the threat of a fine is stronger than no threat at all. And there are many ways in which American states have successfully reduced littering (more on this in a moment). What about those pesky ATVs roaring after midnight? The Scottish law does not permit motorized vehicles on private land, so Vicki wouldn't have that problem. And she wouldn't have problems with hunters, either, since they are not automatically permitted to hunt on private land under a right-to-roam law. So if we had in place a hypothetical American law, modeled on the Scottish law, many of the bad behaviors that Vicki lists would be against the law. Still, there might be a problem with those who skirt the law, or are perhaps unaware of it. And there still might be a problem with litter.

How have other right-to-roam countries dealt with litter on private property? Sweden has had some litter problems. Anna Grundén, a project manager for the Keep Sweden Tidy Foundation, said that concerns about litter were raised in the 1960s. Swedes started traveling to natural places in their cars and bringing with them plastic-wrapped picnic food. These visitors were leaving messes behind, so in 1962, the Swedish Society for Nature Conservation launched the Keep Nature Tidy campaign, which evolved into the Keep Sweden Tidy Foundation, a nonprofit organization. Today, Keep Sweden Tidy organizes mass cleanups and educates the public on the right of public access. The foundation works with 2,700 preschools and elementary schools across Sweden to promote environmental stewardship. They have kids act out plays, such as *Big Eagle Adventure*, in which children pretend to protect a nest from intruders who are trying to steal an egg. For teenagers, the foundation posts YouTube videos and talks about allemansrätten in positive terms. "It was important for us to not be like, 'You can't do that. You can't do that. You can't do that,'" said Grundén. "It was more like, 'Look what you can do. We have these amazing opportunities. But be sensible.'"

In 2016, 767,000 Swedes, or about 8 percent of the Swedish population, participated in the foundation's annual mass cleanup.[347] "We see that these cleanup activities have a positive impact in people's behavior and attitude," said Grundén. "If you've been picking someone else's litter up, you are less likely to litter yourself." A survey from participants in the litter campaign suggests that Grundén is right. Eighty-one percent of the participants agreed that participating in the cleanup increased their knowledge about litter, and 86 percent agreed that the campaign changed their littering behaviors.

Supervision also is a way to reduce littering, but Nils Hallberg, a legal advisor for the Swedish Environmental Protection Agency, said, "Supervision helps people be a bit more cautious, but we don't think that's the right way to work the issue. We think supervision is complementary. The most important part is to kind of create a mindset where the entire population thinks littering is a nasty thing to do in nature."

All the Swedes I talked with said that they remember something from their childhood that encouraged good environmental stewardship. For Hallberg it was Skogsmulle, the wooden troll. "I have vivid memories of their campaign when I was

a child," said Hallberg. "It's an easy message to
grasp. Outdoor kindergarten was a thing that almost every kid went to. You did that for a few weeks.
Or every Saturday for five weeks. They had a sort of
mascot. He looked like a troll. Something from the
fairy tales living out in the woods. This character
was very sad and affected by littering, and all the
kids were supposed to help him gather litter and
clean up nature. There's no one my age who doesn't
have a clear view of what he looks like. There's an
entire generation that has that image clear in mind.
The wooden troll."

Litter is a problem in America. But just because
it's a problem doesn't mean that nothing can be
done about it. Consider cigarette consumption as
an example of a bad habit that we've mostly kicked.
In 1965, 42 percent of American adults regularly
smoked cigarettes.[348] But after decades of tax increases and public service campaigns, the smoking
rate dropped to 21 percent of the adult population
in 2005. By 2015, only 15 percent of us regularly
smoked.[349] Or consider seat belt use. In the early
eighties, only 14 percent of Americans used seat
belts.[350] In 1984, New York passed the first state law
requiring people to wear seat belts. Owing to subsequent state laws in forty-eight more states (New
Hampshire never passed one), as well as decades of
public service campaigns, seat belt use in 2014 was
at an all-time high of 87 percent.[351]

And of course the United States has its own long
history of reducing litter. There's a scene in the TV
show *Mad Men*, set in the sixties, when the Drapers
are having a family picnic in a park. Before getting
in the car to go home, Don thoughtlessly throws a

beer can into the woods, and Betty shakes trash off a picnic blanket. The camera remains on all the trash as the family remorselessly drives off. This vignette of 1960s American culture reminds us that back then we had yet to associate littering with immoral behavior. It was something that even wealthy and educated people did. As in Sweden, Americans in the sixties had cars from which to throw things, not to mention more bottles, cans, cigarette butts, and plastic than they'd ever had. Up until that time, there had been very little public outreach to reduce littering.

The Keep America Beautiful organization was founded in 1953, and it worked to reduce littering through a series of public service announcements, most notably in 1971 with the famous "Crying Indian" commercial.[352] Today, states have their own anti-littering campaigns. One of the most successful is the "Don't Mess with Texas" campaign, which reduced the amount of litter on highways by 72 percent in six years, according to the Texas Department of Transportation. They got Texas celebrities such as Willie Nelson, LeAnn Rimes, and Lance Armstrong to speak out against littering,[353] and they advertised catchy slogans such as, "Your first car was ugly, but Texas doesn't have to be," and "It's Take-Out. Not Toss-Out." In 2007, the Texas Department of Transportation reached out to children by creating the Litter Force, made up of four superheroes who protect Texas scenery from trash villains. "Don't Mess with Texas" has been so successful that 71 percent of Texans know that "Don't Mess with Texas" relates to litter. In 2006, the campaign made the Madison Avenue Advertising Walk of Fame.

This may seem nonintuitive, but there's something to be said for reducing vandalism by increasing public access to a place. This strategy worked at the Callendar Estate, outside of Falkirk, Scotland. The Callendar Estate contains a private mansion as well as six thousand acres of private farm and woodland. In the 1990s, the estate's woods were constantly trashed and set on fire. Local businesses, trying to avoid garbage-handling fees, would come and dump huge piles of trash onto the grounds. In 1992, when Guy Wedderburn took over as the estate's land manager, the estate was so frequently set on fire by young men that he had to employ two people each summer to drive a water tank to put out fires. The estate's solution, up until Wedderburn arrived, was to try to keep people out. But it never worked. Keeping people off of six thousand acres of land was nearly impossible. It was easy for these young men to sneak onto the forbidden estate and make a mess. Wedderburn, though, had an idea. He wanted to see what would happen if he opened up, rather than continued to close off, the estate to the local community. (This was years before the Scottish right of responsible access bill.) "By trying to keep people out, all we were getting were troublemakers," said Wedderburn. "By flipping that horse around and welcoming the public, we found that we didn't get an increase in the problems. We got a decrease in the problems. Ordinary, decent citizens were keeping an eye on things, reporting problems, and generally encouraging better behavior. It was pretty much an unqualified success." The eyes and ears of the local community were critical to decreasing vandalism, said Wedderburn. Another factor was that the trails had begun to look tidy and inviting. Wedderburn reasons that locals were less likely to leave litter or vandalize a natural space that had been "smartened up." Also, by working with the community, local people started to develop a greater sense of responsibility and ownership of their local environment. To them, it was something to be appreciated, not destroyed. As for the water tank, Wedderburn said it's covered in cobwebs. "We found it in the bushes a couple of years ago and both tires were flat. We haven't used it for a long time."

This goes to show that littering can be reduced, even if it will never fully go away. In their laws, England, Wales, and Scotland also have included rights for landowners to temporarily close off their property, ranging from a few days to several weeks. We can imagine giving American landowners these same rights, and perhaps granting them rights to close off areas for much longer periods if they can prove that roamers' behavior is especially destructive. Between public outreach campaigns, the threat of fines, and the landowner's right to close off sensitive property, litter might not be as big a hurdle as many Americans imagine it to be.

Won't landowners start to get sued by injured hikers more often?

Anybody breaking an ankle (or even a toenail) while hiking on somebody's land would sue the landowner faster than you can pronounce the word "lawyer."

—Pete from Hartford

Many landowners post "No Trespassing" signs not to be ornery and unwelcoming but to protect themselves from possible lawsuits. In the legal world, there are three types of people who might walk on your land. The first is an "invitee." These are people whom the landowner has invited onto her land, and there usually is an economic transaction between them. (Perhaps these invitees are hunters who are paying to hunt on the landowner's property.) There is a standard for "reasonable care" for invitees, which means that the landowner must regularly check her property for dangerous conditions. The landowner could get sued by an invitee should the invitee get injured on the landowner's property. The second type of person who might walk on your land is a "licensee." Licensees have an express or implied invitation to be on the landowner's land. Let's say that this licensee is a friend. It's your duty as a landowner to tell your friend about any hazards on your property—things such as slippery rocks, an uncovered well, or a dangerous bridge. To a reasonable degree, the landowner is responsible for the safety of invitees and licensees. The landowner can be sued if, say, one of the guests breaks an ankle by stepping into a well that the guest hasn't been warned about. The third type of person who might walk on your land is a "trespasser." Unlike the other two types, the landowner is not responsible for and, for the most part, cannot be sued by trespassers.[354]

One of the major reasons that landowners put up "No Trespassing" signs is because they are terrified about getting sued by any of the above. Posting such a sign turns licensees into trespassers. If everyone is a "trespasser," then the landowner reduces the likelihood of getting nailed by a costly lawsuit. Society suffers as a result of this situation. Landowners who might like to share their land have reasons not to. The countryside is littered with unwelcoming "No Trespassing" signs. And the general public have far less land that they can legally walk over.

The truth is that landowners are rarely sued for these sorts of things. But occasionally a landowner is sued, word spreads, and suddenly a countryside of landowners are posting "No Trespassing" signs. Consider the case of *Sallee v. Stewart*. In 2010, a woman named Kim Sallee chaperoned a group of kindergartners on a tour of an Iowa dairy farm. Sallee and a group of students were directed to go up to a hayloft, where Sallee fell through a hole in the flooring and broke her leg and wrist. Normally, state recreational-use statutes would protect the welcoming landowners against being sued. But because, in this situation, the landowners played a "supervisory role," they were liable and had to pay for damages. These sorts of loopholes understandably terrify landowners. Iowa landowners asked the Iowa legislature for a stronger recreational-use statute, and they got one. The new statute gives landowners immunity from lawsuits except in cases in which there is a "*willful* or *malicious* failure to guard or warn against a dangerous condition, use, structure, or activity." What might fall under the category of "willful or malicious" that could get a landowner sued? Only the unthinkable. A landmine, a spiked pit, or an old shack booby-trapped with a shotgun. So a strong recreational-use statute is something states can pass now to encourage landowners to open up their lands for recreation and agricultural tourism.

English landowners can sleep easy because the CRoW Act declares that they are not liable for any injury unless they purposefully create a risk for walkers.[355] The law says that no landowner can be sued because of injury due to:

> a risk resulting from the existence of any natural feature of the landscape, or any river, stream, ditch, or pond whether or not a natural feature, or a risk of that person suffering injury when passing over, under or through any wall, fence, or gate, except by proper use of the gate or of a stile.[356]

This means that if a man gets trampled by a cow in a pasture, or if a child drowns in a pond, or if a woman cuts herself badly when hopping over a wall, the landowner will not be held responsible and cannot be sued.

Considering that accidents and injuries often occur in the outdoors, and considering that landowners would go broke if they had to compensate everyone who had an accident on their property, the only way to make the right to roam fair and appealing to landowners (who are no doubt losing a bit of their privacy) would be to borrow from the Iowa and English laws and provide them with the strongest possible protections. It ought to be impossible to sue landowners except in scenarios in which landowners have acted maliciously.

Americans are armed to the teeth

I would be absolutely terrified to roam freely.
Three hundred million guns are also roaming
freely in this country.

—"J" from New Jersey

America, yes, has a lot of guns. And America, yes,
has its share of homicides. According to the most
recent worldwide homicide rates, the United States
is ranked around the middle of all nations, with
about 4.5 homicides a year per one hundred thousand people. In 2014, there were 11,961 homicides
in the United States.[357]

Few, if any, homicides involve landowners and
recreation seekers in the countryside. Only 7.5 percent of American homicides took place in rural areas. Drug-related deaths are mostly contained to
cities (67 percent of the time). The same is true of
gang-related homicides (70 percent of the time).[358]
And most of the time acquaintances and family
members commit these homicides (78 percent of
the time).[359] A stranger killing a stranger accounts
for only 22 percent of all homicides.[360] If these statistics don't relieve your fears, let's search the Lexis-
Nexis archives over the past twenty years for
homicides that involve landowners shooting people
for walking on their land (not to be confused with
landowners shooting people for breaking into and
entering their homes).

For all the posted signs that threaten the lives of
would-be trespassers, there are only a few cases in
which trespassers have actually been shot. In 2009,
a family in Liberty County, Texas, was driving home

from an evening of swimming. When they parked on the side of the road to pee in the woods, they were met with gunfire by nearby homeowners who had put up a homemade sign that read, "Trespassers will be shot. Survivors will be re shot!! Smile I will."[361] Four family members were shot with a twelve-gauge shotgun, including a seven-year-old boy who was hit in the head and died.

In January 2014, two men in West Virginia were shot by sixty-two-year-old Rodney Bruce Black, who fired on them when he saw them shaking the door of a tool shed. Black thought the shed was on his property. It wasn't. It turned out that the two victims had just bought that property and were shot and killed on their own land.[362]

Perhaps the most well-known trespassing tragedy is the case of sixteen-year-old Yoshihiro Hattori, a Japanese exchange student in Louisiana. In 1992, Hattori, who had dressed for a Halloween party as John Travolta from *Saturday Night Fever,* accidentally approached the wrong house and was shot in the chest by homeowner Rodney Peairs. The event sparked an international relations nightmare.[363]

If other trespassing-related homicides have taken place in the middle of a cow pasture, a private forest, or on a private coastline in the past few decades, they are hard to find. And two of the above aren't really relevant to the right to roam. The West Virginia murders took place because the landowner thought his property was being burglarized, and the Louisiana murder with the Japanese exchange student happened in front of a home, not in someone's private woods.

Well, okay, but what about all those hunting-related fatalities? The International Hunter Education Association, which compiled hunting fatality statistics, found that between 1995 and 2001 there were about ninety hunting-related fatalities a year in America, about 30 percent of which were self-inflicted.[364] For the years 1994, 1995, and 1997, the association kept a statistic for people who were shot and killed because they were "mistaken for game"—an annual average of thirty-one people.

Given that there are 324 million Americans, almost 14 million of whom go hunting each year,[365] the thirty-one accidental deaths, not to mention the presumably greater number of nonfatal casualties—as tragic as they are—argue for better hunting safety more than against the right to roam.

One could try to argue that Europeans can get away with the right to roam because they are in gun-free zones. But that's not the case. Of the top ten industrialized Western countries with the most guns per capita, seven are countries with partial or complete right-to-roam systems, including Finland (ranked No. 2, with 34 guns per 100 residents), Sweden (ranked No. 3, with 32 guns), Norway (ranked No. 4, with 31 guns), Austria (ranked No. 7, with 30 guns), Iceland (ranked No. 8, with 30 guns), Germany (ranked No. 9, with 30 guns), and Switzerland (ranked No. 10, with 24 guns).[366] These guns are mostly concentrated in rural countrysides, yet the shooting of people while exercising their right to roam is, to my knowledge, unheard of. (The United States, it should be mentioned, does have absurdly more guns than these other gun-loving countries, with 112 guns per one hundred residents.) Many of these countries have hunting traditions that are just as strong as ours. One out of twenty-four Americans hunt. This is similar to the ratio in Scandinavian countries. According to the European Federation of Associations for Hunting & Conservation, in Denmark, one out of thirty-three citizens hunt. In Norway, it's one out of twenty-four, in Sweden one out of thirty-one, and in Finland one out of seventeen.[367] This all goes to show that armed residents, camowearing hunters, and bearded backpackers *can* harmoniously mix without bloodshed in rural countrysides.

But aren't Americans legally allowed to kill trespassers who walk over our land under toughsounding "Make My Day" statutes and castle doctrine laws? The answer is a definite no. Despite all the unwelcoming signs you see saying, "Trespassers Will Be Shot," no American landowner can legally shoot someone for merely being on their land. The right to kill exists only when a series of circumstances align. For one, an intruder must have broken into someone's home, business, or vehicle. In several states, such as New York and New Jersey, the homeowner has a "duty to retreat" if he can do so safely and if the intruder has not shown aggression. Most states, though, do not require a duty to retreat, but even then, killing an intruder is not always permitted. In Texas, a homeowner cannot kill an intruder unless several circumstances are met: the intruder must enter a home, business, or vehicle; the homeowner must believe that "deadly force is immediately necessary," and lethal force is permitted to protect oneself to "prevent the other's imminent commission of aggravated kidnapping, murder, sexual assault, aggravated sexual assault, robbery, or aggravated robbery."[368] In other words, even tough, gun-wielding Texans cannot kill people just for entering their homes. And they certainly can't kill people just for walking across their llama pastures.

Consider the case of Markus Hendrick Kaarma, a Montana man whose garage had been burglarized a few times. He set a trap by leaving the garage open, installing surveillance equipment, and hanging a purse. A German exchange student entered the trap (his friends said he was looking to steal beer) and Kaarma shot and killed him. Even though Kaarma's home was being invaded and even though it was reasonable to suspect burglary, and even though Montana has a tough-sounding castle doctrine law, Kaarma still was sentenced to a seventy-year prison term.[369] Kaarma could not prove that "force was necessary to prevent an assault upon the person or another then in the occupied structure," which is required under Montana law.[370]

In fact, in all of the fatal shooting cases that I mentioned earlier, the shooter was penalized. It turns out that Rodney Bruce Black, the West Virginia shooter, is a paranoid schizophrenic and has been sentenced to life in a mental institution.[371] Sheila Muhs, who shot the family and killed the little boy on the Texas roadside, was given a life sentence.[372] The shooter in the case of the Japanese exchange student was acquitted, but he was held liable for $650,000 in damages.[373]

While occasional trespassing-related shootings do occur, they are not legal, and they are extremely rare. Fortunately for right-to-roamers, the stereotype of the foul-mouthed, gun-wielding American landowner who shoots on site just isn't accurate. I learned from my own trespassing adventures that landowners are more likely to greet you with a hearty hello and a jug of water than the red dot of their rifle scope.

We should stick to recreation on public land, or just create more public land

Trying to establish free roaming areas in the US would be a battle I would not pick. There are national parks, state parks, and city walking paths that are available to everyone, and much safer if you have the need to roam. That is where I would start.

—Dennis Scanlon from Minnesota

I deal with the inadequacy of our national parks and public lands extensively in Chapter 6, but to sum up:

- The great majority of our public lands are in Alaska and other western states, areas with some of the smallest populations.

- We have reached a point where the creation of more big national parks is unlikely. We can hope for a handful of new national parks in the future, but they will be small, about the size of new parks such as South Carolina's 26,500-acre Congaree National Park (2003) and California's 26,600-acre Pinnacles National Park (2013). It's also likely that future national parks will merely be converted into parks from existing national monuments. This means that we won't really be gaining any more roamable public land; the designations of existing public land will merely be changed. We cannot expect the federal estate to significantly grow, especially with a growing population and expanding urban development. Designating new national parks, anyway, is an extremely expensive way of creating recreation space.

• Though our public spaces provide world-class recreation opportunities, they fail to do something that only the right to roam can achieve, which is to give people a green, quiet, and natural space near their home, whether they live in a city, town, or suburb. Our national parks, for most people, are an unreasonably long drive away.

People want to keep private land to themselves

Private property is just that: private. Keep out or suffer the consequences. This is not rocket science.

—Paul from White Plains

This is a simple but strong argument. Many landowners do not want to share their space and possibly compromise their privacy. As I've already argued, though, the right to roam—or the "right of responsible access" (whatever we want to call it)—can be compatible with private property. Even if the right to roam is given to the public, the landowner still owns her land, can develop it as she pleases, and can engage in an assortment of economic activities on it. Plus, under a well-defined code (more on this in the next chapter) her privacy would be protected.

Plus, for landowners, there is much to gain from the right to roam. They can gain greater immunity from lawsuits, for example. And landowners, of course, can roam, too. Even a landowner who owned 49 percent of the entire country would benefit, because she would gain the freedom to roam over the other 51 percent.

Consider just how many people don't own land or own very little land. There are about 39 million Americans (or 12.4 percent) who live in apartments, according to the US Census Bureau's 2015 American Community Survey.[374] Almost all of these apartment-dwellers own no land, and if they have access to land of their own then it's probably a small lawn that they share with fellow tenants. People who own their own houses probably don't own a lot of land, either. Consider just how many of us live in towns, villages, boroughs, and cities, where people probably have little more than a small lawn for themselves. These places are what the US Census Bureau calls "incorporated places," a designation that does not include people living in suburbs and exurbs. According to the Census Bureau, 198 million people, or 62.7 percent of the US population, live in incorporated places, yet this group occupies only 3.5 percent of the US land area.[375]

In Scotland, one of the reasons why the right to roam was accepted by rural landowners was because Scotland's rural landowners acknowledged that the rural parts of the country are heavily subsidized by the urban areas, where most of the country's tax revenue is generated. "It wasn't tenable for land managers who were in receipt of large amounts of taxpayer funding to be able to say to people, 'Get off my land,'" said Rob Garner, the access and policy advisor for Scottish Natural Heritage. "Land managers weren't really in a position to speak as if the land was their back garden."

While the rural United States may not be as subsidized as rural Scotland, urban states in the United States generally subsidize the rural states. According to a study by the Tax Foundation, for every dollar that the urban state of New Jersey pays in taxes, it gets back only sixty-one cents in federal spending and benefits. For every dollar the rural state of Wyoming pays in taxes, it gets back $1.11. (The top five "shortchanged" states are New Jersey, Minnesota, Illinois, Colorado, and Massachusetts. And the top five states that get more federal tax money than they pay are Wyoming, Alaska, North Dakota, Hawaii, and South Dakota.)[376] A 2012 Pew Research Center survey found that rural Americans were more likely to benefit from federal benefit programs (Social Security, Medicare, Medicaid, food stamps, welfare, or unemployment benefits) than urban Americans. Sixty-two percent of rural Americans received at least one of these benefits, according to Pew, compared with 54 percent of suburban Americans and 53 percent of urban Americans.[377] Each year, taxpayers give $20 billion in annual subsidies and insurance to farmers.[378] Between 2010 and 2016, federal agencies annually spent between $1.3 billion and $2.1 billion of taxpayer money on rural fire suppression. Americans' tax dollars are often used to protect private property in rural America—private property that these taxpayers are more than likely forbidden from accessing.[379]

The same urban-to-rural payments are happening in state budgets, too. A 2010 report from Indiana showed that the consolidated City of Indianapolis and Marion County sends about $420 million more to the state than it receives each year. A 2009 study showed that the Atlanta metro area paid 61 percent of Georgia's taxes but got only 47 percent of it back.[380]

In many parts of the country, we see a rural population that benefits from urban taxes. These urban taxes are helping to pay for rural road repair, rural Social Security, rural crop subsidies, and other rural services. Because urban people send much of their tax money to rural America, I believe urban people have a reasonable claim on rural land. The roads and bridges that lead to a homeowner's country estate may well have been paid for with city people's taxes. Since rural areas are money deprived, and since crowded cities are nature deprived, it follows that some kind of trade would be fair.

———

Paul from White Plains may believe that property is not "rocket science," but it's not simplistic, either. Property, as we've seen, is an institution that has evolved over thousands of years. The United States continues to urbanize, and the more people we have living in urban environments, the more we will, as a country, be obliged to live with more rules on how we can and cannot use our land. In other words, regulation—which has become a dirty word to many Americans—is nevertheless an everyday part of urban life, simply because in urban life regulation is more necessary. The more we live in cities, the more we will become comfortable with land-use restrictions and claims on individuals by the community. In 1950, 64 percent of Americans lived in urban areas.[381] In 2014, it was 81 percent.[382] The United Nations report "World Urbanization Prospects" projects that between 2015 and 2050, the United States can expect a steady decline in our rural population, from 60 million people to 50.5 million people.[383] During that same time frame, the United States can expect a huge increase in our urban population, from 265 million people to 350 million.[384] By 2050, the report estimates that the United States population will be 87 percent urban.[385] At this rate, how urban will we be by 2100? By 2150? Think of how much of the electorate, by then, will be dominated by urban ways of thinking. Plus, with all these folks living in cities, we can anticipate a greater demand for access to the green spaces that cities lack.

There are urban demographic trends that may push us toward the right to roam, and there are also trends in property and environmental law. Property law scholar Harvey Jacobs points to a pattern in property law that shows an emergence of community power. Since the first Earth Day in 1970, we have imposed restrictions on farmlands, shorelands, and wetlands, including the Clean Water Act and Clean Air Act, and the Endangered Species Act. "Do those owners always gripe [when we impose a new law]? Absolutely," said Jacobs. "But is the broad-term trend one where the owner is having to yield to the community and continual renegotiations? Yes."

Between a growing urban population that is comfortable with land-use regulations and a steady stream of environmental laws that restrict land use for the sake of the environment and the greater community, we might expect, in the future, conditions that will make the right to roam, as well as more ecology-friendly regulations, not only possible but realistic.

The laws of Europe do not apply to the United States

Newsflash: We aren't Europe. If you want to live in a place like Europe, move to Europe.

—Mike Damone

While a few proud Americans might argue that America has no use for the inventions, customs, and laws of Europe, we might remind ourselves that our country was founded on the principles of Greek democracy, Roman republicanism, the Scottish Enlightenment, and English law. Our language is European, our country is named after an Italian, and our war of independence was financed by the French. Americans have benefited from Alan Turing's computer, Edward Jenner's smallpox vaccine, and Florence Nightingale's modern nursing. And we've made use of polyester fabric, the armored tank, the periodic table, the theory of evolution, and the miracles of Viagra. Many an American is guilty of having lounged on Swedish furniture while drinking Dutch beer and watching reruns of *Downton Abbey*. We have borrowed from Europe in the past, and it's okay to borrow from Europe again, for we still have much to learn. After all, while laws have borders, ideas don't.

CHAPTER 8

The Right to Roam—How Do We Get There?

Our age is retrospective. It builds the sepulchres of the fathers. It writes biographies, histories, and criticism. The foregoing generations beheld God and nature face to face; we, through their eyes. Why should not we also enjoy an original relation to the universe? Why should not we have a poetry and philosophy of insight and not of tradition, and a religion by revelation to us, and not the history of theirs? Embosomed for a season in nature, whose floods of life stream around and through us, and invite us by the powers they supply, to action proportioned to nature, why should we grope among the dry bones of the past, or put the living generation into masquerade out of its faded wardrobe? The sun shines to-day also. There is more wool and flax in the fields. There are new lands, new men, new thoughts. Let us demand our own works and laws and worship.

—Ralph Waldo Emerson, "Nature," 1836

Before we talk about the nuts and bolts of turning an idea into law, let's first remind ourselves of the obvious. Our country is troubled with problems that

stand in the way of basic governance: political polarization, how we finance political campaigns, the
widespread distrust of government. To obtain the
right to roam, Americans would need to both solve
these issues and become more like Europeans, who
tend to support laws passed in the public interest.
Or we would need to become more like previous
generations of Americans, who also once believed
in governing for the common good.

When we look at the countries that have the
strongest right-to-roam laws and customs—Scotland,
Sweden, Norway, and Finland—we see a group of
countries that have achieved what we might call a
sort of democratic magnificence. Their governments
tend to be more functional. Their democracies are
stronger. And their citizens have expansive rights
to health care, education, and social security. We
probably won't see the right-to-roam movement in
a poor country like Zimbabwe, or in a country with
deplorable human rights like Iran. There may not
be a stronger push for roaming rights in the United
States until other fundamental needs are met. As
we've seen, the English rambling clubs didn't start
their mass trespasses and their crusades for access
rights until they secured their ten-hour workday and
five-day workweek.

If we were to place "roaming rights" on Maslow's
hierarchy of needs for a country, then roaming
rights might appear near the tippy-top of the
pyramid—one of the most difficult rights for a nation to realize. Achieving a certain degree of governmental, cultural, and economic magnificence
may first be necessary. This book and certainly this
author are unable to prescribe solutions to all of our

nation's problems, so for our needs, it may be best
to simply put aside the political realities and incon-
veniences of the day and imagine that our nation
will one day again entertain bold initiatives and
champion grand ideas, and that our government
will, as difficult as it may be to imagine, competently
and civilly perform its duties.

Zoning

For this section, I've interviewed a number of property law scholars to get their take on whether they
think the right to roam is constitutional (most agreed
it is) and how it could be legally implemented. John
Lovett is a property law scholar at Loyola University
and an expert on the Scottish right-to-roam law. He
believes that the best way to institute the right to
roam is to start small, on the local and state level. A
municipality could, for instance, include the right
to roam in its zoning regulations. This might be the
most effective approach, said Lovett, because the
United States has a long history of recognizing zoning ordinances (dating back to 1916 in New York
City).[386] A zoning ordinance will often require a
landowner to build her home a certain distance
from the edge of her property or limit the height of
buildings in certain areas. Yet zoning ordinances
do not require paying landowners any compensation. In zoning, there's an understanding that these
kinds of use restrictions create reciprocal advan-
tages for all similarly situated property owners in
the community. Even if a landowner loses the right
to determine all uses of her property, she benefits

because other properties in the area are subject to
the same restrictions, and these restrictions benefit
all property owners in the community. "If we were
to graft a right of responsible access in a zoning
ordinance, one could argue plausibly that all property owners in the community would similarly gain
a reciprocal advantage," said Lovett, "because we
would have recreational access on all of our neighbors' property."

Lovett said that as things are today, though, a
state law giving citizens the right to roam would
probably be declared unconstitutional in the courts
because they tend to take a highly formalistic view
of the right to exclude. In other words, courts would
probably say—unfortunately, in Lovett's view—that
a right of responsible access is more intrusive than
a setback requirement or a height restriction because it generally denies the property owner the
right to exclude nonowners. But let's imagine a state
law, anyway, and see how it might work.

State laws and state amendments

To institute the right to roam, Eric Freyfogle, a property law scholar at University of Illinois at Urbana-
Champaign and the author of *On Private Property*,
recommends passing a state law that authorizes local
governments to undertake land use regulation. The
law would give communities the choice to open certain types of land for public use. This way, towns
and counties can decide for themselves whether they
want to open up land. This may be better than having the state government force all localities to accept

a potentially undesired law. "There certainly could be areas where the majority of the people are supportive of it," said Freyfogle. "And if it got tried out in a number of areas and the ill effects are not what people feared, and if public enthusiasm builds up, then it might work."

Brian Sawers, a property law scholar, said that the safest way to get the right to roam would be for a state to amend its state constitution. This removes the possibility of a state court getting in the way if it were to declare a right-to-roam law unconstitutional. Resistance from state courts isn't just a hypothetical scenario. In the past, both the Maine and Massachusetts state legislatures have wanted to expand public access to their coasts. In 1986, Maine's legislature enacted the Public Trust in Intertidal Land Act, which allowed people to walk the beach up to the high tide mark (the wet sand). But the Maine Supreme Judicial Court ruled the law unconstitutional.[387]

The way to get around an uncooperative state supreme court is to safeguard the right to roam by amending a state constitution. This method isn't without precedent. Pennsylvania's 1683 colonial constitution gave its residents the right to hunt, fish, and fowl on "all other lands therein not inclosed." Vermont's 1777 state constitution gave the "liberty to hunt and fowl, in seasonable times, on the lands they hold, and on other lands (not enclosed)."[388] The writing in the current Vermont constitution is about the same today, and in Vermont you have a right not only to hunt, fish, and fowl on private land but also to use unposted land for hiking and other recreational purposes. This makes Vermont—legally at least—perhaps the most roamable state in the union.[389]

A state could just pass a state law that permits walking on private land and simply hope that the state court won't declare the law unconstitutional. Many states already have some recreation-friendly laws. Brian Sawers writes that most states consider land "open" until a landowner takes action to close off access. Twenty-nine states define *trespass* as something that happens only when a person walks on posted or fenced private land. In other words, walking on unposted and unfenced private land in these twenty-nine states is perfectly legal, unless the landowner personally notifies the hiker or puts up a sign.

Other states have granted impressive rights for the use of coastlines. In a New Jersey Supreme Court case, the court ruled that the public's rights to use the coasts are "not limited to the ancient prerogatives of navigation and fishing, but extend as well to recreational uses, including bathing, swimming and other shore activities."[390] Hawaii and Oregon give the public coastal access up to the vegetation line.

Other states—such as Minnesota, Maine, and New Hampshire—don't have right-to-roam laws, but there are at least local customs that make it unpopular for landowners to exclude. In South Dakota, hunters are allowed to hunt on "section lines" (the lines that divide farms) regardless of whether there's a road there or not. In the Dakotas and in Montana, all streams, rivers, and lakes are public property (though it can be difficult for people to get to waters that are trapped behind private-property boundaries). All states, as I mentioned in a previous chapter, have recreational-use statutes, which give landowners protection from frivolous lawsuits.

But none of these states go far enough to provide recreational access to their residents. In all fifty states, the landowner still has an incredible amount of power. In any state, a landowner can, except in a handful of situations, shut off his land from the rest of the country. Even in Vermont, landowners can opt out of the roaming culture if they post enough signs. And while it's great that Hawaii and Oregon have open coasts, other states—such as Delaware, Maine, Massachusetts, Pennsylvania, and Virginia—use the mean low-tide line to mark the edge of a landowner's property. In some of these states, the landowner owns all the way down to the water at low tide. In Maine, Massachusetts, and Virginia, the coasts are mostly privately owned, according to the Surfrider Foundation.[391]

What's needed for the twenty-first century and beyond is a strong right-to-roam law. The Scottish law is a good model for states in the United States. It's better than the convoluted English law, which offers access to only certain types of lands and which permits only a few select activities. And the Scottish law is more helpful than the Swedish system because the Swedish system exists more as a custom. A custom isn't enough and would not work very well in the United States, where a law is needed to clearly give rights. The Scottish Outdoor Access Code is well over one hundred pages and is far too long to include here. But let's look at this lightly edited and Americanized summary of the Scottish code, which might serve as a good rough draft for a law:

1. Everyone, of whatever age or ability, has access rights. But you only have access rights if you exercise them responsibly.

2. You can exercise these rights over most land and inland water in the United States, including mountains, deserts, woods and forests, grasslands, margins of fields in which crops are growing, paths and trails, rivers and lakes, the coasts, and most parks and open spaces. Access rights can be exercised at any time of the day or night.

3. You can exercise access rights for recreational purposes (such as pastimes, family and social activities, and more active pursuits such as horse riding, cycling, camping, and taking part in events), educational purposes (concerned with furthering a person's understanding of the natural and cultural heritage), some commercial purposes (where the activities are the same as those done by the general public), and for crossing over land or water.

4. Existing rights, including public rights of way and navigation, and existing rights on the foreshore, continue.

5. The main places where access rights do *not* apply are:

- houses and lawns, and non-residential buildings and associated land;

- land in which crops are growing;

- land next to a school and used by the school;

- sports or playing fields when these are in use and where the exercise of access rights would interfere with such use;

- land developed and in use for recreation and where the exercise of access rights would interfere with such use;

- places like airfields, railways, telecommunication sites, military bases and installations, working quarries, and construction sites; and

- visitor attractions or other places that charge for entry.

6. Local authorities can formally exempt land from access rights for short periods. Local authorities and some other public bodies can introduce their own local laws.

7. Access rights do not extend to:

- being on or crossing land for the purpose of doing anything that is an offense, such as theft, breach of the peace, nuisance, poaching, allowing a dog to bother livestock, dropping litter, polluting water, or disturbing certain wild birds, animals, and plants;

- hunting, shooting, or fishing;

- any form of motorized recreation or passage (except by people with a disability using a vehicle or vessel adapted for their use);

- anyone responsible for a dog that is not under proper control; or to

- anyone taking away anything from the land for a commercial purpose.[392]

Here we see a rough outline for a possible law. In short, residents would be able to walk and camp and take part in other outdoor activities, day or night, over private woods, pastures, and farmland that is not in use. We could consider this law the "floor" of what's allowable. Local governments could add rights to the law, such as the right to pick wild berries. This would be the law's "ceiling." And it would be up to private landowners to decide if they want to welcome hunting, fishing, and ATV riding on their properties.

Under this Scottish-inspired law, it would no longer be legal to put up signs and erect fences for the sole purpose of excluding people from recreational spaces (except to keep people out of one's home and surrounding yard). As we've seen, Scotland doesn't like to refer to their system as the "right to roam," but as the "right of responsible access," which is to say that there is no right of access without public responsibilities. The hiker or camper or birder, then, would have a series of rules that outline their responsibilities, as well as fines, penalties, and jail time to face if these rules are not followed.

Landowners would be given strong protections from getting sued (except in cases in which they've willfully and maliciously created hazards). And, like the English and Scottish landowners, American landowners would have the right to shut down their land temporarily for reasons of fire prevention, conservation, and land management.

If we agree that the Scottish system makes the most sense, we can also copy how they fund their system and solve conflicts of interest. The Scottish pay out ten million dollars annually to thirty-two local authorities, each of which appoints an access officer and schedules local access forums, where representatives from various interest groups (for example, farmers, hikers, and access officers) find solutions to common problems. In the United States, we can imagine, say, the State of New York distributing funds to local governments to perform these functions.

Is the right to roam a "taking?"

There is a debate among scholars over whether the right to roam constitutes a "taking." A taking, according to the Takings Clause of the Fifth Amendment, occurs when the government takes private property for public use. If the right to roam *is* a taking, then the right to roam is unconstitutional, unless the government provides monetary compensation to landowners. Paying all the landowners in America would be a burden on taxpayers. But if the right to roam is *not* a taking, then taxpayers do not have to compensate landowners.

Eric Freyfogle, the author of *On Private Property*, said that a right-to-roam law that applied broadly to private lands should not amount to a taking of private property under current Supreme Court precedent. A taking automatically occurs, he points out, if a law allows an outsider to use part of a private parcel *and* if the landowner is denied all use of that particular part. This was the situation in the *Loretto* decision, mentioned in an earlier chapter. But a right-to-roam statute would leave landowners free to use all of their lands, excluding them from nothing. The only other way a landowner can claim a taking, Freyfogle said, is if a statute singles out one or a few landowners for a burden that other landowners do not have to bear. In other words, if a law opens up the lands of only one owner, then the owner likely deserves compensation. This was the situation in the *Kaiser Aetna* ruling, also mentioned earlier. Only one landowner in that dispute had to open its marina to public use. Again, though, a well-drafted right-to-roam statute would apply much more broadly to all owners of particular types of land within a political jurisdiction, so the "singling out" rationale wouldn't apply. "A lot of people have misinterpreted these cases," said Freyfogle in an interview with me. "They think that if the government allows public access, then somehow that's automatically a taking. But that is clearly not what the Supreme Court has said." By most standards, Freyfogle notes, a right-to-roam statute really is quite a modest burden on rural landowners. They remain free to use their lands as they see fit, and the economic impact on them would typically be very modest, much less than the impacts of countless urban land-use regulations. Indeed, he points out, many rural landowners would have real trouble offering proof that a right-to-roam statute has decreased their land values. "Unless we have a fetish about the right to exclude," Freyfogle claims, "a Scottish-style right of responsible access ought to be constitutional under current case law, given its minimal interferences with landowner activities."

Harvey Jacobs, a property law scholar, agrees that a right-to-roam law isn't a taking because under a right-to-roam law, nothing is actually being taken. "It's still the landowner's land," said Jacobs. "He gets to do what he wants to do with his land." In other words, the public would only be *using* the landowner's land under the right to roam; no one and no government is actually *taking* that land. The land is still possessed by the landowner.

As the country changes, what was legislatively unimaginable becomes imaginable. "We can point again and again and again to property rights your grandmother or great-grandfather had that you do not have," said Jacobs. "And they didn't get compensated when it was taken." What Jacobs is saying is that the Constitution is interpreted differently by different generations, who are affected by changes in cultural attitudes and values, and new scientific and technological breakthroughs. The right to roam, in other words, may be constitutional; it just depends on which generation is interpreting the Constitution when we start legislating the right to roam.

Jacobs said that it is more than possible that we'll have the right to roam in our future. Property has changed in significant ways in just the past one hundred years or so. As early as the beginning of the twentieth century, a landowner could claim "the heavens above" his land. But ever since airplanes, the heavens are no longer exclusively owned by landowners. In this same period, husbands more or less owned their wives, parents owned their children, and farmers owned their animals. But advances in women's rights, child labor laws, and animal rights have changed our understanding of ownership. "A man can no longer beat his spouse, send his children off to work in the mines or the mills, or mistreat his horse simply with the claim that 'they are mine, and I will do what I want with them,'" said Jacobs.[393]

"Could it happen in the US?" Jacobs said about the right to roam. "Absolutely. There is absolutely nothing in US property law which stands as a conceptual or practical impediment to the realization of the right to roam. Absolutely nothing that would in theory prevent it from being realized." To Jacobs, the more important question is whether our social values and cultural feelings over private property will evolve to allow us to see land the way many Europeans see it today. Let's remember that our values from the founding of our country up until the Civil War were oriented toward serving the common good (of white Americans, at least), so much so that early Americans could mine for ores and militias could cut down private trees on private property. Practicality was partly to blame for the cultural shift in this country away from roaming toward a system of exclusionary private property. But practicality, in a different form, may very well shift us back in the other direction as our population grows, urbanizes, and undergoes cultural changes that we can't foresee.

Let's return to the Takings Clause for a moment. Based on existing Supreme Court rulings, the right to roam, we've established, is not a taking. But can we not imagine a situation in which a landowner deserves compensation? I would argue that if a landowner suffers a distinct harm—more than ordinary landowners (such as with a decreased land value)—then that landowner deserves to be compensated. We can certainly imagine such a situation. Perhaps this landowner owns private land with a special natural feature, like a waterfall. Or perhaps she owns picturesque land next to a city. These places could be swamped with sightseers, and her land value could plummet. This would constitute a distinct harm that deserves compensation.

That said, for places only *somewhat* affected by the right to roam, it's often the case that land values *rise* when a new public trail or cycle path is opened up nearby. Many people, especially young people, seek out homes that have a nearby path, whether for commuting or recreation. Trails and bike paths have increased house price premiums in San Antonio, Austin, Ohio, Delaware, Washington, and Indianapolis, according to an analysis by Headwaters Economics, a nonprofit.[394] One rails-to-trails conversion—the High Line in New York City—caused resale values of properties near the trail to increase 10 percent faster than properties just blocks away.[395] In other words, increased foot traffic doesn't automatically lead to decreased land values and a lower quality of life. Sometimes it has the opposite effect.

A national law and a federal amendment

Why don't we pass a single national law, the way the English, Welsh, and Scottish did? The problem with a national right-to-roam law in the United States is that the federal government doesn't have much control over property law. That is a power that has historically been left to the states.

Brian Sawers, an academic at Emory University, believes that the right to roam is likely to be interpreted as a taking, and the only way around the obstacles presented by the Fifth Amendment is to change the US Constitution with a federal amendment. This is probably the most implausible route to the right to roam, but since it's theoretically possible, we ought to at least consider the idea. Besides, a proposed right-to-roam amendment is not altogether unheard of. The right to roam in the

American colonies was so important that the Pennsylvania delegation to the Constitutional Convention proposed an amendment to the Bill of Rights that read:

> The inhabitants of the several states shall have liberty to fowl and hunt in seasonable times, on the lands they hold, and on all other lands in the United States not inclosed, and in like manner to fish in all navigable waters, and others not private property, without being restrained therein by any laws to be passed by the legislature of the United States.[396]

In what may seem to the modern reader to be a rather theatrical disapproval of the proposed Constitution, the Pennsylvania delegation disclosed worries about a government made up of "harpies of power" who would "have no congenial feelings with . . . perfect indifference for . . . and contempt of" the people. These harpies would "prey upon the very vitals . . . and riot on the miseries of the community."[397]

The right to roam was clearly so cherished in Pennsylvania that the Pennsylvania delegation wanted it to be a part of the US Constitution and forever protected by the US government. The Pennsylvania delegation's right-to-roam amendment did not get enough support and their wish never came true. No right to roam, right to hunt, right to fowl, or right to fish made it into the US Constitution. If the Pennsylvania delegation had gotten their wish, then perhaps we would think differently about private property and our collective rights over it. Nevertheless, the Pennsylvania delegation gave us a helpful legal precedent that we can build on, albeit more than two hundred years later.

Amending the Constitution requires a two-thirds majority in the House and Senate, as well as ratification from three-fourths of the states. Federal amendments can transfer power from the states to the federal government, as in the case of alcohol consumption. Before the Eighteenth Amendment (the one that prohibits alcohol) was ratified in 1919, states got to choose whether their state was wet or dry. The Eighteenth Amendment, which would eventually be reversed, transferred the power to prohibit the manufacture and sale of alcohol from the states to the federal government.

A right-to-roam amendment would have to address two things. For one, it would have to say that all Americans have the right to roam. Two, it would have to give power to Congress to define the right to roam. Congress would then pass a law that would probably give the powers to create a regulatory framework to the Secretary of the Interior, who would adjust the regulations as needed, rather than force Congress to pass a bill every time changes were needed. The regulations could very well look something like the lightly edited Scottish code above.

———

But let's not venture too deep into the legal weeds here, especially over an unlikely federal amendment. The course of action we choose to take will be up to future members of the US Congress, or the fifty different states, each of which has its own unique geographical character and legal challenges, not to mention the particular needs and concerns of its residents.

There are many more-immediate goals to meet and smaller steps to take before we plan for something as grand as a constitutional amendment. As a country we simply must start talking about access rights. There are many magazine pieces and doctoral dissertations that need to be written to expand our knowledge of the subject. A Right to Roam Society ought to be formed to fight to keep land open. Our local swimming holes and cemeteries must be protected. We can support statewide groups that promote access to our beaches. And, more than anything, we need to just get out and walk, feel a connection to the land, and pass these values down to our children. Only a society that walks will fight for the right to walk.

CHAPTER 9

This Land Is Our Land

Conservation is a pipe-dream as long as Homo
sapiens *is cast in the role of conqueror, and his
land in the role of slave and servant. Conservation becomes possible only when man assumes the
role of citizen in a community of which soils and
waters, plants and animals are fellow members,
each dependent on the others, and each entitled
to his place in the sun.*

—Aldo Leopold, 1947[398]

In 1689, English philosopher John Locke, in his *Two
Treatises of Government,* built a theory of how private
property originates. Property, Locke said, comes
into a man's possession when he mixes his labor with
the land. Locke's views on property justified the
Euro-American conquest of the New World, which
Native Americans hadn't mixed their labor with, at
least in the ways that the European settlers accepted.
With our three hundred years of hindsight, we can
safely criticize Locke for not coupling his theory
with a sense of empathy for the Native Americans,
who were about to be dispossessed of their lands.
But his theory, at least from the perspective of the

British Empire and the American colonists, was practical, useful, and made sense. Locke's theory articulated the notion that land didn't need to be granted from the Crown; it could just be obtained through labor.[399] In time, the North American wilderness would be colonized, privatized, and cultivated. Locke did what needed doing: He presented a theory of property for the needs of his era.

If Locke's labor-mixing theory made sense for the British in the seventeenth century, what might be a good theory for Americans in the twenty-first? I'd like to argue that our current theory of private property—in which one person may exclude whomever he pleases and may generally use the land however he likes—is outmoded and inadequate. The fundamental problem is that this theory has been built on a foundation of flawed philosophies—philosophies gathered from some of the darkest corners of American history. America's system of absolute and exclusive ownership of land comes from our Dominionist religion, which tells us that it's our right to subdue and rule over the land. It comes from our dog-eat-dog capitalist economy, in which the richest of us get to accumulate and control most of the land, money, and power. It comes from our hardy individualist mythology, which would have us believe that individual liberty is more important than the common good. It comes from early Americans' belief that America will forever be abundant in lands and resources, a belief that we've somehow managed to carry into the twenty-first century, when our lands and resources are becoming increasingly scarce.

Radical ranchers draw on this cultural inheritance to seize public land. Industrial farmers feel like they have license to leave nitrates in our waters. Antisocial landowners are empowered to close off our swimming holes and cemeteries. This is no odd quirk of Americana. This is part of who we are, down to our marrow. Our religion, our economy, our cultural mythology claim dominion over everything, from the languishing microbes in our deep soils up into the heavens of our gassed troposphere.

So when we build our own twenty-first-century theory of property, it would be wise not to build it on a foundation of false mythologies, selfish economics, and cherry-picked religious verses. Perhaps we can build our theory on much firmer ground: the science of ecology.

Ecosystems are made up of complex, interdependent relationships between environments and the organisms that live within those environments. When someone who doesn't understand the land's ecology manages the land, then the ecosystem and all of its inhabitants become threatened. According to Aldo Leopold—arguably the principal ecologist of the twentieth century—our system of private property is in serious need of reorganization, more so than any other element of society.[400] "The average citizen," wrote Leopold, "especially the landowner, has an obligation to manage his land in the interest of the community, as well as his own interest . . . The nation needs and has a right to expect the private landowner to use his land with foresight, skill, and regard for the future."[401] Leopold wanted to expand the boundaries of community "to include soils, waters, plants, and animals, or collectively: the land." This is part of his "land ethic," which he hoped would change "the role of Homo sapiens from conqueror of the land-community to plain member and citizen of it."[402]

We are, as Leopold argued, connected to the fertility of our soils, the cleanliness of our air, and the billions of microorganisms, insects, and animals that give us life. Land is in our food, our blood, our cells. Land is in our clothes, our vehicles, our lives. We are connected to not just our own and our neighbors' lands. We are connected to land all across America: from California's vegetable valleys, to the Great Plains' aquifers, to the South's timberlands, to the Midwest's dairy farms, and to New England's apple orchards. What happens in one region affects the others. And it's not just our nation's lands that we are connected to, for we are also connected to the air quality in China, where factories manufacture our devices. We are connected to the jungles of South America, where deforestation accelerates global warming. We are connected to the ice shelves of Antarctica, where the continent's meltwater slowly floods our coasts. We are connected to the oil of the Middle East, which lubricates our consumer-capitalist machine. And we are connected to the peoples of all countries, for we all, to varying degrees, spout into the atmosphere greenhouse gases, together writing our millennium's great environmental drama, of which we don't yet know the end. Our clothes, our products, our lifestyles—everything we do and use and own—connect us to these faraway peoples and faraway places. And yet we manage to see ourselves as isolated beings—"America First" hardy individualists—separate from not only the biotic kingdom but from our fellow man.

Because our lives are connected to everyone else's, we need property laws that better reflect humanity's shared reliance on, destruction of, and ownership of the globe. Looking ahead to the future, with our environmental problems and with the impacts of climate change set to dramatically alter life on our planet, we need a system of property that is better grounded in not just morality and justice but also in science.

John Stuart Mill said that "the land of every country belongs to the people of that country."[403] This is a thought to be admired, and Mill, as usual, was ahead of his time. But I'd like to extend his ethic in Aldo Leopold–like fashion: The land of every country belongs not just to the people of that country but to all of humankind. The land belongs not just to humankind but to the future generations of humankind. The land belongs not just to future generations of humankind but to all living things and the ecosystems on which they rely. Let's not be so fixated on something as small as individual liberty—to exclude and do whatever we wish—when we should be thinking about something far grander and far nobler: the health of the community, the health of the planet, the prosperity of the human race and all our fellow species. There is nothing that convinces me that land should ever wholly and despotically belong to one person. Our laws must reflect our more truthful and scientific relationship to the land, for we are but small members in the congress of living things, and the power we have wielded has for too long been dominant and disproportionate.

But before our laws can change, our ethics must. Perhaps it'll take a revolution in ethics to sufficiently change our relationship with property. Yet, if anything's worth working toward, is this not it? Could we come to think of the land as the Paiute do—as something that's fundamentally unownable, and as something that's sacred and worthy of our reverence and deserving of our most deliberate care? As suitable a belief system as the Paiute's may be for the environmental challenges of the twenty-first century and beyond, the answer is "probably not." But isn't there at least enough worthwhile content in America's cultural DNA for us to imagine a more communitarian understanding of property taking hold? While America has the institution of private property, dating back to 1623, we also have the egalitarian values of the Revolution and the Founders. We have the great philosophical, scientific, and literary works of Thoreau, Muir, Carson, Dillard, and the rest of our great heroes and heroines of nature. We have the arc of the moral universe, which has been bent toward justice by the arms of our civil rights, gay rights, and women's rights movements. And we have the legacies of all who have lived on our great American landscape, over which animals roamed for millions of years, and into which our Native American forebears etched footpaths and horse trails that were forgotten only a hundred years ago. With all these intertwining cultural and historical DNA strands, can we not also find in our country's heart space for a theory of ownership that is less rigid, less individualistic? I speak of a style of ownership that is more shared—shared with a community that gets to make collective decisions about the land; shared with countrymen and women who value its natural environments; and shared with other life forms that have their own right to exist and thrive. Perhaps we don't need to go as far as the Paiute, who see their families and their histories in the land (though that would do just fine). But so long as we place ourselves in our rightful position within the great chain of life, I'd like to think our relationship with the land will be more sustainable, our lives more enriched, our country's soul more pure.

For the twenty-first century and beyond, I'd like for us to do away with our old theories of property and build a Woody Guthrie theory of property—a theory that claims that this land is your land, my land, or, to put it better, our land.

———

In February of 1940,[404] folk singer Woody Guthrie traveled by bus and thumb from Texas to New York City, where he wrote the lyrics to "This Land Is Your Land." The song became one of the most popular songs in American history. For decades, it has been sung by schoolchildren across the country. It has been borrowed for presidential campaigns and used in airline commercials. Lady Gaga sang parts of it in a Super Bowl halftime show. It has become something of a secondary national anthem.

Guthrie wrote the song in response to Irving Berlin's "God Bless America,"[405] which painted a rosy, and therefore only partial, picture of America in the Great Depression. The original lyrics to "This Land Is Your Land," on the other hand, set out to capture both the country's great inequity and its great promise.

Guthrie had two critical verses that didn't make

it into the popular recordings. Yet even within the common lyrics lies a pretty radical message: the idea that America's land is both yours and mine.

> *This land is your land, This land is my land*
> *From California to the New York island;*
> *From the red wood forest to the Gulf Stream waters*
> *This land was made for you and me.*

We possess this land. It's been made for *us*. There is nothing in his lyrics that indicates that Guthrie was simply referring to our national parks or our public lands. He is talking about much more: our valleys, deserts, farmland—all our country from California to New York. When we sing Guthrie's song, we do not sing it with deference to a rigid system of private property. We do not sing it to glorify landowners' rights to exclude whomever they want. We do not sing it with submission to threatening and unwelcoming "No Trespassing" signs. No, we sing it as free people who feel a sense of collective ownership of our country's lands and waters.

If you think I may be reading too much into the lyrics, then consider Guthrie's rarely sung fifth verse, which was discovered by a Smithsonian archivist in 1997:

> *As I went walking I saw a sign there*
> *And on the sign it said "No Trespassing."*
> *But on the other side it didn't say nothing,*
> *That side was made for you and me.*

Guthrie's radical verse, along with the rest of his sweeter-sounding but still pretty radical song, presents a vision of an America in which Americans, despite whatever differences exist among us, are equal in our right to roam our land, to enjoy our countryside, and to share our nation's natural resources. The song is popular no doubt because it has a catchy tune and a patriotic message, but there is something alluring about the song's populist undertones. There is something pagan in its reverence for natural beauty. There is something cooperative in its theme of shared resources. It is, at its heart, a people's song. When we sing it in a crowd, we can't help but feel close to each other. For the span of the few minutes needed to sing it together, the song makes us feel like a country that shares rather than competes, a country that is generous rather than self-serving, a country that protects rather than exploits. The song makes us feel like we're all in it together.

In January 2009, at the Lincoln Memorial, Pete Seeger and Bruce Springsteen sang "This Land Is Your Land" before a gigantic crowd at President Obama's inauguration. Seeger sang Guthrie's original lyrics, with all six verses, including the one about disobeying "No Trespassing" signs. For a moment, we were a country of roamers, if not in foot then surely in spirit.

I'd like to have us all feel this way. Not just for the duration of a song but for the next many chapters in the great American story.

From Country Meadows to the Alaska tundra, from our rolling grasslands to our industrial farmlands, from New England's apple orchards to North Carolina's Piedmont, from Pennsylvania's Rock Cemetery to Oregon's Malheur Refuge, I'd like to argue for living up to a radical thought that silently dwells in many an American's heart, but which rings loudly in schoolrooms across the country: This land was made for you and me.

It's ours. And we should all get to roam it.

Acknowledgments

I'd like to give a special thanks to my friend David Dalton. It was at his dinner table where the idea for this book was hatched, and it was in his home where I wrote most of the book. Without his encouragement, edits, and review, this book would not have been possible. I'd also like to thank my parents for their support in helping me get over an unfortunate wrist injury while I wrote the book.

I'd like to thank all the scholars, researchers, and professors who took time out of their busy schedules to talk with me and to review my work. A special thanks goes to Eric Freyfogle for his scholarship and thoughtful review. And another to Brian Sawers for his work, review, and our many interviews.

I'd like to thank Kate Conto of the Ramblers, Nigel Curry, and Jerry Anderson for their interviews and reviews, and for helping me comprehend the English and Welsh CRoW Act. A special thanks to Klas Sandell for his research on Sweden's allemansrätten, and for taking the time to review my work. Thank you Nils Hallberg, Anna Grundén, Filippo

Valguarnera, and Peter Fredman for additional help on Sweden's allemansrätten. Thank you Malcolm Combe for dealing with my many questions about Scotland. And thank you John Lovett, Katrina Brown, Rob Garner, Guy Wedderburn, and Simon Craufurd for your help on the Scottish right of responsible access. Thank you Harvey Jacobs, Joel Brammeier, Charles Geisler, Jess Gilbert, and John Gibson for interviews and help with research on property ownership in the US.

I'd like to thank my editor at Blue Rider Press, Brant Rumble, for the edits and encouragement. I'd like to thank David Rosenthal for giving me the opportunity to publish this book, and Scott Alexander for an admirable copy edit. And thanks to everyone at Penguin Random House for making this book possible. I'd like to give a special thanks to Amy and Peter Bernstein, my agents, who've been with me all along and who are my rocks of stability in the stormy waters of the publishing industry.

I'd like to thank my friend Michael Flatt—without your edits this book would be far less readable. I'd like to thank Shelby Smith, Antonia Malchik, and Dean C. Smith for their thoughtful reviews. I'd like to thank Duke University for letting strangers and alums like me make use of your libraries.

Thank you to everyone else who answered my questions through email, talked with me over the phone, and whose scholarship made this book possible. Lastly, thank you to all of the people who have protected American land and who have fought to make it accessible.

Further Reading

Jerry Anderson, "Britain's Right to Roam: Redefining the Landowner's Bundle of Sticks," *The Georgetown International Environmental Law Review,* 19 (2007).

Eric Freyfogle, *The Land We Share: Private Property and the Common Good* (Washington DC: Island Press, 2003).

Eric Freyfogle, *On Private Property: Finding Common Ground on the Ownership of Land* (Boston: Beacon Press, 2007).

Eric Freyfogle, *A Good That Transcends: How US Culture Undermines Environmental Reform* (Chicago: University of Chicago Press, 2017).

Eric Freyfogle, *Our Oldest Task: Making Sense of Our Place in Nature* (Chicago: University of Chicago Press, 2017).

Andro Linklater, *Owning the Earth: The Transforming History of Land Ownership* (New York: Bloomsbury, 2013).

John A. Lovett, "Progressive Property in Action: The Land Reform (Scotland) Act 2003," *Nebraska Law Review,* 89 (2011).

Richard Pipes, *Property and Freedom* (New York: Vintage Books, 1999).

Dan Rubinstein, *Born to Walk: The Transformative Power of a Pedestrian Act* (Toronto: ECW Press, 2015).

Brian Sawers, "The Right to Exclude from Unimproved Land," *Temple Law Review* 83 (2011).

Marion Shoard, *A Right to Roam* (Oxford: Oxford University Press, 1999).

Rebecca Solnit, *Wanderlust: A History of Walking* (New York: Penguin, 2001).

Notes

Numbers in the first column below correspond to note superscripts in the text.

1   *It is not in the nature*: E. O. Wilson, *The Creation: An Appeal to Save Life on Earth* (New York: W. W. Norton, 2006), 12.

2   *My first years*: Luther Standing Bear, *Land of the Spotted Eagle* (Lincoln: University of Nebraska Press, 2006), 260.

3   *Between 1990 and 2010*: "New York: 2010. Population and Housing Unit Counts," US Census Bureau, 2012, 28, https://www.census.gov.

4   *forty-one million acres of American forest*: "Development of Non-Federal Rural Land 2007," USDA, http://www.nrcs.usda.gov.

5   *The organization Smart Growth America*: "Dangerous by Design 2014," Smart Growth America, 1, http://www.smartgrowthamerica.org.

6   *Americans walked an average*: Tara Parker-Pope, "The pedometer test: Americans take fewer steps," *New York Times,* October 19, 2010.

7   *far fewer than the averages*: David Bassett Jr., Holly Wyatt, Helen Thompson, John C. Peters, and James

O. Hill, "Pedometer-measured physical activity and health behaviors in US adults," *Medicine & Science in Sports & Exercise* 42 (2010): 1822–23.

8   *According to a 2012 study*: Pedro C. Hallal, Lars Bo Andersen, Fiona C. Bull, Regina Guthold, William Haskell, and Ulf Ekelund, "Global physical activity levels: surveillance progress, pitfalls, and prospects," *The Lancet* 380 (2012): 247–57.

   The Guardian assembled the country-by-country data on a Google Docs spreadsheet. Of 120 countries studied, the United States was ranked the forty-seventh most sedentary country.

9   *National Center for Health Statistics*: "Health, United States, 2016," National Center for Health Statistics, 221.

10 *"through the woods and over the hills"*: Henry David Thoreau, "Walking," *The Atlantic*, 1862.

11 *Consider how many of these places*: Jess Gilbert, Spencer D. Wood, and Gwen Sharp, "Who Owns the Land? Agricultural Land Ownership by Race/Ethnicity," *Rural America* 17 (2002): 56.

12 *97 percent of agricultural landlords are white*: "Farmland Ownership and Tenure: Highlights," USDA, September 2015, 3.

13 *In 1978, the data showed*: Charles Geisler, "Trophy Lands: Why Elites Acquire Land and Why It Matters," *Canadian Journal of Development Studies* 36 (2015): 9.

14 *has seen its wealth inequality*: Drew DeSilver, "US income inequality, on rise for decades, is now highest since 1928," Pew Research Center, December 5, 2013.

15 *CEOs saw a 941 percent*: Lawrence Mishel and Jessica Schieder, "CEOs make 276 times more than typical workers," Economic Policy Institute, August 3, 2016.

16 *the wealthiest .1 percent own*: Emmanuel Saez and
    Gabriel Zucman, "Wealth inequality in the United
    States since 1913: Evidence from capitalized income
    tax data," National Bureau of Economic Research,
    2014, 1.

17 *According to* The Land Report: *The Land Report*,
    Winter 2016. Calculations of the top landowners
    and their portion of total land and total private
    land are my own.

18 *There are 766 million acres of forest*: Sonja N. Oswalt and
    W. Brad Smith, "US Forest Resource Facts and
    Historical Trends," Forest Service, August 2014, 7 & 14.

19 *the population owned 53 percent*: Geisler, "Trophy
    Lands," 10–11.

20 *Corporations, trusts, and other owners*: "Farmland
    Ownership and Tenure," USDA. From table titled
    "Acres owned by farm operators, operator
    landlords, and non-operator landlords, 2014," last
    modified April 10, 2017.

21 *In 2016, there were a record 331 million visits*: Katia
    Hetter, "America's most popular national parks
    are . . ." CNN, March 10, 2017.

22 *The four agencies*: "Federal Land Ownership:
    Overview and Data," Congressional Research
    Service, December 29, 2014.

23 *US census projections*: Sandra L. Colby and
    Jennifer M. Ortman, "Projections of the Size
    and Composition of the US Population: 2014 to
    2060," US Census Bureau, March 2015.

24 *A 2012 report by the US Forest Service*: "Future of
    America's Forests and Rangelands: Forest Service
    2010 Resources Planning Act Assessment," USDA,
    August 2012, 11.

25 *If we opened up the portion of our country*: The numbers
    of croplands and grassland pasture come from the
    "Major Uses" study from the USDA: Cynthia

Nickerson, Robert Ebel, Allison Borchers, and Fernando Carriazo, "Major Uses of Land in the United States, 2007," USDA, December 2011, i. The forest numbers come from "Forest Resources of the United States, 2012" from the USDA: Sonja N. Oswalt, W. Brad Smith, Patrick D. Miles, and Scott A. Pugh, "Forest Resources of the United States, 2012," USDA, October 2014, 6.

26 *"One does not sell the earth"*: Dee Alexander Brown, *Bury My Heart at Wounded Knee* (New York: Sterling, 2009), 308.

27 *The computer game*: Guild Wars Nightfall: Dattatreya Mandal, "10 of the Biggest Open-World Video Games Released in Terms of Map Size," *Hexapolis,* November 5, 2014.

28 *Jehovah gave us verdant hills*: Walt Mason, "Keep off," *El Paso Herald,* May 12, 1919.

29 *The Dovins decided to permit access*: Karen Shuey, "Owners of Caernarvon Township cemetery sue to keep people from visiting," *Reading Eagle,* August 11, 2016.

30 *Referring to having to rebury her son*: Linda Hervieux, "Keep out! Loved ones told cemetery is off limits," *Newser,* August 12, 2016.

31 *Hundreds of Hawaiians claimed*: Alex Heath, "Mark Zuckerberg is suing hundreds of Hawaiians to protect his 700-acre Kauai estate," *Business Insider,* January 19, 2017; Alex Heath, "'People are furious down here': Hundreds of protesters will amass at Mark Zuckerberg's Hawaiian wall," *Business Insider,* January 26, 2017.

32 *Zuckerberg's neighbors called*: Harriet Alexander, "Mark Zuckerberg's Hawaii neighbours angered by 'monstrosity' wall around estate," *Telegraph,* June 28, 2016.

33 *For decades, families in Laurel County, Kentucky*: Nita Johnson, "Springing a tradition . . . Residents

concerned about new owner's policy," *Sentinel Echo*, September 12, 2016.

34 *After a forecast*: Patricia Doxey, "In Saugerties and elsewhere, authorities cracking down on swimming hole trespassers," *Daily Freeman*, September 9, 2016.

35 *Sometimes these closures prevent people*: Laura Donovan, "No more hiking to the scenic Medicine Hole," *Bismarck Tribune*, June 23, 2014.

36 *In Winston-Salem, North Carolina*: Tim Clodfelter, "Ask SAM: No trespassing signs on greenway?" *Winston-Salem Journal*, February 24, 2016.

37 *In Duluth, Minnesota*: John Myers, "Landowner kicks Superior Hiking Trail off property," *Duluth News Tribune*, April 26, 2015.

38 *Around Avila Beach in California*: Cynthia Lambert, "Couple who fenced off Ontario Ridge trail to get cease-and-desist order," *The Tribune*, July 11, 2014; Rhys Heyden, "Fencing furor: As a popular hiking trail is fenced off, stakeholders clash over land-use rights," *New Times*, February 3, 2014.

39 *In Lancaster County, Pennsylvania*: Colin Deppin, "Protest picnic, mass trespassing scrapped in energy company, park patron dispute," *Penn Live*, May 13, 2016.

40 *Florida's constitution says*: Jane Costello, "Beach access: Where do you draw the line in the sand?" *New York Times*, January 21, 2005.

41 *In Clearwater, Florida*: Charlie Frago, "Clearwater City Council asked to wade into beach access dispute," *Tampa Bay Times*, November 22, 2013.

42 *Now the only way*: Frago, "Our View: Court ruling on Harpswell beach access shows need for public land," *Portland Press Herald*, November 30, 2016.

43 *A local, Kevin Hendrickson*: Erik Lacitis, "Lake City residents fight to regain use of now-private beach," *Seattle Times*, June 28, 2015.

44   *In Hampton, Virginia*: Robert Brauchle, "Va. Supreme Court: Grandview land owner can keep people off beach property," *Daily Press,* June 8, 2015.

45   *In Milford, Connecticut*: Thomas Ebersold, "Beach fence gets ZBA approval: The full story," *Milford Mirror,* March 10, 2016; Bill Coleman, "Letter: Resident fights to keep fence off Woodmont beach," *Milford Mirror,* March 4, 2016.

46   *In another Malibu incident*: Devon McReynolds, "Malibu's Paradise Cove busted for charging for public beach access . . . again," *LAist,* July 3, 2016.

47   *In Rye, New Hampshire*: Elizabeth Dinan, "Binnie: Friendly neighbors shouldn't lose property rights," *Sea Coast Online,* July 3, 2016.

48   *In Westerly, Rhode Island*: Richard Salit, "Judge rules in favor of landowners; public has no right to roam stretch of Misquamicut shore," *Providence Journal,* September 5, 2014.

49   *In Honolulu, Hawaii*: Bridgette Namata, "Residents up in arms over blocking of public access to beach," KHON2, January 10, 2015.

50   *in Hawaii, the public*: Katie Tannenbaum, "Surfrider Foundation's Stance on Beach Access," Surfrider Foundation, last modified on May 28, 2017, http://beachapedia.org/Beach_Access.

51   *In Sea Bright, New Jersey*: Linda Ocasio, "Longing for a day at the Shore: Public access is elusive at many New Jersey beaches," *Newark Star Ledger,* June 23, 2013.

52   *in Massachusetts*: Nelson Sigelman, "Gone fishin': Has Martha's Vineyard gone to the dogs?" *MV Times,* July 29, 2015.

53   *Near San Francisco, California*: Adam Nagourney, "It's privacy vs. the people in the battle for Martin's Beach," *New York Times,* June 15, 2014; Georgia

Wells, "Billionaire Vinod Khosla seeks $30 million
to let beachgoers cross his property," *Wall Street
Journal,* February 29, 2016.

54   *In Maine, Massachusetts, and Virginia*: Tannenbaum,
"Surfrider Foundation's Stance on Beach Access."

55   *the 1981 movie* On Golden Pond: "Golden Pond is
now open to the public," *New York Times,* September
8, 1999.

56   *As of today, there is one access point*: Squam Lakes
Association, Recreation Map, https://www
.squamlakes.org/.

57   *In Long Beach, Indiana*: "Judge rules lakefront
property owners can't keep public off Lake
Michigan beach," NBC Chicago, July 30, 2015.

58   *In Webster, New York*: Sarah Taddeo, "Beach owners,
boaters at odds again," *Democrat and Chronicle,*
August 12, 2014.

59   *Mayor Joseph Polisena*: Tim Forsberg, "Debate over
Oak Swamp Reservoir access heats up," *Johnston
Sunrise,* May 19, 2016.

60   *Despite there being few bodies of water*: "Nevada Court:
Tahoe Beach is private, not public," KOLO8,
November 11, 2014.

61   *In Wisconsin Dells*: Jeff Smith, "Upham Woods:
Opponents of fenced-off river site sound off at town
hall meeting," *Wisconsin Dells Events,* May 27, 2016.

62   *In the Adirondacks of New York*: Brian Mann,
"Adirondack paddling lawsuit goes to highest court,
giving landowners hope," North Country Public
Radio, March 25, 2016.

63   *These streams are the property*: Dan Boyd, "Gov.
Martinez signs bill into law restricting NM stream
access," *Albuquerque Journal,* April 3, 2015.

64   *John Gibson, the president*: Kelley Christensen,
"Update: Montanans increasingly kept out of public

land, report says," *Montana Standard*, September 12, 2014.

65   *The BLM says that about 9 percent*: "Public Access to BLM Managed Public Lands: A Report to the House Appropriations Committee," August 2004, 3.

66   *He is on the record saying*: Brett French, "Governor announces Montana public land access initiatives," *Missoulian*, June 9, 2016.

67   *In Washington State*: Sanjay Bhatt, "Weyerhaeuser is buying Plum Creek for $8.4B to form timber giant," *Seattle Times*, November 8, 2015.

68   *They charge $300 for motorized access*: Tom Paulu, "Weyerhaeuser changes fees, permits for forest access," *The Columbian*, May 23, 2016.

69   *For five months a year*: Reed Kaestner, "Huge California ranch offers public access for a price," *Orange County Register*, July 5, 2016.

70   *In 1980, while on the campaign trail*: James Coates, "'Sagebrush Rebellion' on hold, group lights other legal fires," *Chicago Tribune*, March 16, 1986.

71   *"I believe God gave"*: Ryan Bundy, Certificate of Conferral, Multnomah County Detention Center, July 2016.

72   *But behind the waving flags*: Anthony McCann, "Malheur," *LA Review of Books*, September 7, 2016.

73   *After a pipe broke*: Curtis Skinner, "FBI finds trench of human feces at cultural site on Oregon refuge," Reuters, February 17, 2016.

74   *In 1879, 350 Paiute endured*: Leah Sottile, "'Who knows what they're stomping on?': Tribe worried about Ore. refuge artifacts," *Washington Post*, January 17, 2016.

75   *They turned to Facebook for help*: Joe Quigley, "Send snacks," *Daily Kos*, January 4, 2016.

76 *Living in their bubble*: Tay Wiles, "Malheur occupation, explained," *High Country News*, January 4, 2016.

77 *In 2015, Senate Amendment 838*: Logan Graham, "The American public land heist: from North Carolina beaches to rural Oregon," *Technician*, September 12, 2016.

78 *Three other bills*: "Across the Country," Outdoor Alliance, http://www.protectourpublicland.org.

79 *This will lead to increased resource production*: "Keep Our Wild in public hands," Wilderness Society, http://wilderness.org.

80 *Senator Ted Cruz*: Claire Moser, "Ted Cruz launches Senate fight to auction off America's public lands," *ThinkProgress*, July 10, 2014.

81 *"Two percent of [Texas]"*: Rocky Barker, "Ted Cruz says Feds should dump public land," *Idaho Statesman*, March 5, 2016.

82 *There have been more than fifty bills*: Michael Caranci, "Keep public lands in public hands," *Record Searchlight*, September 16, 2016.

83 *The Wilderness Society*: "Keep Our Wild in public hands," Wilderness Society, http://wilderness.org.

84 *That means that the places*: Max Greenberg, "Idaho has sold off 1.7 million acres of land to private interests," Wilderness Society, May 2, 2016.

85 *Western states already have sold*: Greenberg, "Idaho has sold off 1.7 million acres of land to private interests," Wilderness Society.

86 *Three-hundred and ninety-one acres*: Jacob Klopfenstein, "Utah sells Comb Ridge land to private bidder," *Durango Herald*, October 25, 2016.

87 *The new landowners*: Brian Maffly, "Lyman Family Farm blocks road to popular part of new Bears Ears monument in Utah," *Salt Lake Tribune*, January 5, 2017.

88 *The new landowners immediately blocked*: Klopfenstein, "Utah sells Comb Ridge land to private bidder."

89 *In California*: Jean Trinh, "Snooty beachfront homeowners who block beach access to us commoners will be fined," *LAist*, June 23, 2014.

90 *Christie was properly chastised*: Nick Corasaniti, "'That's him': Christie goes to the shore, and the critics pounce," *New York Times*, July 3, 2017.

91 *There is nothing which so generally*: William Blackstone, *Commentaries on the Laws of England (1765–1769)*, Book 2, Chapter 1.

92 *The enclosure bill of 1869*: Simon Fairlie, "A Short History of Enclosure in Britain," *The Land*, 2009.

93 *In 1815, Parliament had given power to magistrates*: Rebecca Solnit, *Wanderlust: A History of Walking* (New York: Penguin, 2001).

94 *Of the Peak District's 150,000 acres*: Dave Renton, "Peak District, 24 April 1932," *Socialist Review*, April 1999.

95 *They even used telescopes*: Benny Rothman, *The Battle for Kinder Scout: Including the 1932 Mass Trespass* (Altrincham: Willow Publishing, 2012).

96 *Four hundred ramblers*: Rothman, *The Battle for Kinder Scout*, 21.

97 *"private property in land is a bold"*: Peter Linebaugh, *Magna Carta Manifesto: Liberties and Commons for All* (Berkeley: University of California Press, 2008), 220.

98 *"You are lost if you forget"*: Eric Freyfogle, *The Land We Share* (Washington DC: Island Press, 2003), 4.

99 *Sparta, according to Plato*: Richard Pipes, *Property and Freedom* (New York: Vintage Books, 1999), 5–6.

100 *He believed that produce*: Marion Shoard, *A Right to Roam* (Oxford: Oxford University Press, 1999), 115.

101 *"The first and highest form"*: Pipes, *Property and Freedom*, 7.

102 *In* Politics, *Aristotle*: Aristotle, *Politics*, 350 BCE, http://classics.mit.edu.

103 *Chief Crowfoot of the Siksika*: Martin Adams, *Land: A New Paradigm for a Thriving World* (Berkeley: North Atlantic Books, 2015).

104 *Massasoit, a Wampanaog tribal leader*: Andro Linklater, *Owning the Earth: The Transforming History of Land Ownership* (New York: Bloomsbury, 2013), 25–26.

105 *With these early societies in mind*: Linklater, *Owning the Earth*, 100. From *The Communist Manifesto*: "In this sense, the theory of the Communists may be summed up in the single sentence: Abolition of private property."

106 *Jefferson believed that small landholdings*: Linklater, *Owning the Earth*, 209.

107 *He imagined a nation of sturdy*: John G. Sprankling, *Understanding Property Law*, 20.

108 *"Cultivators of the earth"*: To John Jay, August 23, 1785. From "Letters of Thomas Jefferson," accessed on Yale Law School's The Avalon Project.

109 *Jefferson borrowed from Locke*: Linklater, *Owning the Earth*, 190.

110 *"Whenever there is in any country"*: Thomas Jefferson to James Madison, October 28, 1785.

111 *Jefferson was all for breaking up*: Eric Freyfogle, *On Private Property: Finding Common Ground on the Ownership of Land* (Boston: Beacon Press, 2007), 16.

112 *the top hundred American landowners*: The Land Report, Winter 2016.

113 *Facebook CEO*: Alexander, "Mark Zuckerberg's Hawaii neighbours angered by 'monstrosity' wall around estate."

114 *According to Richard Pipes*: Pipes, *Property and Freedom*, 92.

115 *According to calculations*: Pipes, *Property and Freedom*, 93. Pipes referenced: Colin Clark and Margaret Haswell, *The Economics of Subsistence Agriculture* (London: Macmillan, 1964), 26–27.

116 *In Alaskan Inupiat culture*: Jared Diamond, *The World Before Yesterday: What Can We Learn from Traditional Societies?* (New York: Penguin, 2013), 42.

117 *The Dani of western New Guinea's*: Diamond, *The World Before Yesterday*, 45.

118 *The !Kung Bushmen*: Diamond, *The World Before Yesterday*, 46.

119 *In the Great Basin*: Diamond, *The World Before Yesterday*, 44.

120 *The Code of Hammurabi*: Pipes, *Property and Freedom*, 77.

121 *The Judeo-Christian tradition*: Adams, *Land*.

122 *Augustine of Hippo said*: Shoard, *A Right to Roam*, 117.

123 *In Leviticus 23*: Linklater, *Owning the Earth*, 26.

124 *Islam incorporated a similar view*: Linklater, *Owning the Earth*, 26.

125 *Muhammad said that*: Adams, *Land*.

126 *"a more rational method of exploitation"*: Pipes, *Property and Freedom*, 89.

127 *In England and Wales*: "Call for action over 'deplorable' paths," BBC, June 22, 2002.

128 *The commons were an integral part*: Fairlee, "A Short History of Enclosure in Britain."

129 *The commons, writes Hartmut Zückert*: David Bollier and Silke Helfrich, eds., *The Wealth of the Commons: A World Beyond Market and State* (Amherst: Levellers Press, 2012). Chapter by Hartmut Zückert.

130 *Although some citizens*: Jerry Anderson, "Britain's Right to Roam: Redefining the Landowner's Bundle

of Sticks," *The Georgetown International Environmental Law Review*, 19 (2007): 391.

131 *celebrate folk customs*: Bollier, *The Wealth of the Commons*.

132 *"a busy theatre"*: Shoard, *A Right to Roam*, 105–06.

133 *In 535 CE, Roman Emperor Justinian*: David Bollier, *Think Like a Commoner: A Short Introduction to the Life of the Commons* (Gabriola Island: New Society Publishers, 2014), 87.

134 *Rome would hold no power*: Bollier, *Think Like a Commoner*, 88.

135 *Charter of the Forest*: Bollier, *Think Like a Commoner*, 89.

136 *The English period of enclosure*: Anderson, "Britain's Right to Roam," 383–84.

137 *"the insubordination of commoners"*: Anderson, "Britain's Right to Roam," 383–84.

138 *"dim and distant Parliament"*: Anderson, "Britain's Right to Roam," 386.

139 *"surrounded by hether"*: Anderson, "Britain's Right to Roam," 386–87.

140 *In the early 1600s, radical peasants*: Fairlee, "A Short History of Enclosure in Britain."

141 *The Black Act created fifty offenses*: Fairlee, "A Short History of Enclosure in Britain."

142 *Fields and woodlands*: Shoard, *A Right to Roam*, 109.

143 *land that had been open for millennia*: Shoard, *A Right to Roam*, 326.

144 *In 1824, Reverend Robert Slaney*: Shoard, *A Right to Roam*, 108.

145 *"bug-ridden and verminous houses"*: Shoard, *A Right to Roam*, 180.

146 *Kinder Scout trespasser Jimmy Jones*: "Scout's honor," *The Guardian*, April 16, 2002.

147 *"I am aware that I represent the villain"*: Renton, "Peak District."

148 *Sooner than part from the mountains*: Anderson, "Britain's Right to Roam," 401.

149 *Germany allows walking*: Brian Sawers, "The Right to Exclude from Unimproved Land," *Temple Law Review* 83 (2011): 687–88.

150 *Naturally, with such a countryside*: Anderson, "Britain's Right to Roam," 382.

151 *In England and Wales*: Anderson, "Britain's Right to Roam," 381.

152 *Natural England, a public body*: "Summary of evidence: Access and engagement," Natural England, March 10, 2015, 2.

153 *Today, two-thirds of the United Kingdom's land*: Heidi Gorovitz Robertson, "Public Access to Private Land for Walking: Environmental and Individual Responsibility as Rationale for Limiting the Right to Exclude," *The Georgetown International Environmental Law Review* 23 (2011): 214.

154 *mountain, moor, heath, down, and common land*: Countryside and Rights of Way Act 2000, 2, http://www.legislation.gov.uk.

155 *opened up 3.4 million acres*: Jonathan Klick and Gideon Parchomovsky, "The Value of the Right to Exclude: An Empirical Assessment," *University of Pennsylvania Law School Faculty Scholarship* (2017): 942.

156 *such as the downs in West Yorkshire*: Anderson, "Britain's Right to Roam," 407.

157 *Marine and Coastal Access Act*: Marine and Coastal Access Act 2009, 1, http://www.legislation.gov.uk.

158 *This coastline includes cliffs*: Klick and Parchomovsky, "The Value of the Right to Exclude," 942.

159 *So paddling a canoe on a river*: John A. Lovett, "Progressive Property in Action: The Land Reform (Scotland) Act 2003," *Nebrasha Law Review*, 89 (2011): 785.

160 *They cannot post misleading signs*: Anderson, "Britain's Right to Roam," 408.

161 *Conflicts are rare*: J. H. Lawton, "Red Grouse Populations and Moorland Management," *British Ecological Society* 2 (1990): 15.

162 *The government's analysis*: Anderson, "Britain's Right to Roam," 405–06. Original numbers: £.06 per hectare on seldom visited lands to £8.70 per hectare.

163 *In the summer of 2017*: "Taking Forward Wales' Sustainable Management of Natural Resources," June 21, 2017, https://consultations.gov.wales.

164 *Dr. James Hunter*: Shoard, *A Right to Roam*, 304.

165 *tragedy known as the Clearances*: Lovett, "Progressive Property in Action," 772–73.

166 *"Our family was very reluctant"*: Arthur Herman, *How the Scots Invented the Modern World: The True Story of How Western Europe's Poorest Nation Created Our World and Everything in It* (New York: Three Rivers Press, 2001), 303.

167 *"The land is our birthright"*: James Hunter, *Skye: The Island* (Edinburgh: Mainstream Publishing, 1996), Chapter 10.

168 *Half of Scotland is owned*: Community Land Scotland, http://www.communitylandscotland.org.uk/; Alison Elliot, John Watt, Ian Cooke, and Pip Tabor, "The Land of Scotland and the Common Good," Land Reform Review Group, May 2014, 159.

169 *Paul McCartney and Ian Anderson*: Lovett, "Progressive Property in Action," 771.

170 *It made the land available for*: Lovett, "Progressive Property in Action," 786.

171 *A Scot can therefore*: Lovett, "Progressive Property in Action," 777–78.

172 *The annual cost for the Scottish government*: Interview with Rob Garner, March 2017. £8.1 million equals about $10 million.

173 *Implementing the system*: Lovett, "Progressive Property in Action," 780.

174 *You also can't damage property*: Lovett, "Progressive Property in Action," 787.

175 *This basically means*: Malcolm Combe, "Get off that land: non-owner regulation of access to land," *Juridical Review* (2014): 287.

176 *American law scholar John Lovett*: Lovett, "Progressive Property in Action," 777–78.

177 *Hikers, then, are free to walk*: Lovett, "Progressive Property in Action," 782–83.

178 *Trump built a wall*: Katrin Bennhold, "In Scotland, Trump built a wall. Then he sent residents the bill," *New York Times*, November 25, 2016; Severin Carrell, "Trump golf course staff photographed urinating woman 'to detect crime,'" *The Guardian*, April 4, 2017; Rob Edwards, "Police accused Trump resort of getting access law wrong," *The Ferret*, January 31, 2017.

179 *It's even prohibited to let hedges*: Land Reform Act 2003, 14 (1), http://www.legislation.gov.uk/asp/2003/2.

180 *After an initial ruling*: Malcolm Combe, "Access to Land and to Landownership," *Edinburgh Law Review*, 14 (2010): 106.

181 *The sheriff ruled that*: Lovett, "Progressive Property in Action," 814.

182 *Landowners can temporarily close off*: Lovett, "Progressive Property in Action," 788.

183 *Landowners can close off land*: Lovett, "Progressive Property in Action," 789–90.

184 *Landowners take issue with walkers*: Bill Slee, Katrina Brown, Kirsty Blackstock, Peter Cook, John Grieve, and Andrew Moxey, "Monitoring and Evaluating the Effects of Land Reform on Rural Scotland: A Scoping Study and Impact Assessment," *Scottish Government Social Research* (2008): 43.

185 *"Any time someone tries"*: Interview with Malcolm Combe, March 2016.

186 *In 2005 and 2006, the association honored Scotland*: "Oregon and Scotland earn top marks on IMBA report card," *Cycling News*, December 23, 2006.

187 *The 7stanes district*: "Economic value of mountain biking in Scotland," *Scottish Enterprise*, April 2009, 31.

188 *In 2009, annual income*: "Economic value of mountain biking in Scotland," 9.

189 *A 2010 study conducted by Scottish Natural Heritage*: D. M. Bryden, S. R. Westbrook, B. Burns, W. A. Taylor, and S. Anderson, "Assessing the Economic Impacts of Nature Based Tourism in Scotland," Scottish Natural Heritage commissioned report (2010): i.

190 *"I'm trying to create a business model"*: Interview with Simon Craufurd, April 2017.

191 *According to a Scottish recreation survey*: Slee et al., "Monitoring and Evaluating the Effects of Land Reform on Rural Scotland," 42–43; "Scotland's People and Nature Survey 2013–2014," Scottish Natural Heritage, 1.

192 *Fifty percent of survey respondents*: "Scotland's People and Nature Survey 2013–2014," Scottish Natural Heritage, 1.

193 *The urban population now makes up*: "National Records of Scotland, 2009," using the Scottish Government Urban Rural Classification 2009–2010, http://www.gov.scot.

194 *fishing and hunting*: Anna Sténs and Camilla Sandström, "Allemansrätten in Sweden: A Resistant Custom," *Landscapes* 15 (2014): 106–07.

195 *Vandals can be fined*: Richard Campion and Janet Stephenson, "The 'right to roam: lessons for New Zealand from Sweden's allemansrätt," *Australasian Journal of Environmental Management* 17 (2010): 21.

196 *Sweden saw far fewer*: Robertson, "Public Access to Private Land for Walking," 220–22.

197 *Rather than specific legislation*: Campion and Stephenson, "The 'right to roam,'" 20–22.

198 *Anna Sténs and Camilla Sandström*: Sténs and Sandström, "Allemansrätten in Sweden: A Resistant Custom," 115.

199 *Many landowners acknowledged*: Janet Stephenson and Richard Campion, "Recreation on private property: landowner attitudes towards allemansrätt," *Journal of Policy Research in Tourism, Leisure and Events* (2013): 10.

200 *The Federation of Swedish Farmers*: Stephenson and Campion, "Recreation on private property," 6.

201 *One of the landowners interviewed*: Stephenson and Campion, "Recreation on private property," 11.

202 *In 2004, of the twelve thousand respondents*: Thomas Beery, "Nordic in nature: friluftsliv and environmental connectedness," *Environmental Education Research* 19 (2013): 99–100.

203 *Eighty percent of respondents said allemansrätten*: Klas Sandell, "The Right of Public Access in Sweden," presented at "Nordic Rural Futures: Pressures and Possibilities" carried out by the Department for Urban and Rural Development, Swedish University for Agricultural Sciences and the Swedish National Rural Network, May 3–5, 2010, 3.

204 *Even the people in the countryside*: Sandell, "The Right of Public Access in Sweden," 5.

205 *Studies show that over 90 percent*: Peter Fredman, Mattias Boman, Linda Lundmark, and Leif Mattsson, "Economic values in the Swedish nature-based recreation sector, a synthesis," *Tourism Economics* 18 (2012): 905.

206 *nature-based tourism industry*: Fredman et al., "Economic values in the Swedish nature-based recreation sector," 906.

207 *In a survey of nature tourism businesses*: Klas Sandell and Peter Fredman, "The Right of Public Access: Opportunity or Obstacle for Nature Tourism in Sweden?" *Scandinavian Journal of Hospitality and Tourism* 10 (2010): 301.

208 *In 2017, Visit Sweden*: "Freedom to roam," Visit Sweden, https://visitsweden.com.

209 *In a national survey*: Sandell and Fredman, "The Right of Public Access in Sweden," 4.

210 *Many Swedish schools are nature schools*: Beery, "Nordic in nature," 96–98.

211 *"wildest, leafiest, and least trodden way"*: John Muir, *A Thousand-Mile Walk to the Gulf* (New York: Penguin, 1992), 2.

212 *he called the entrance to Horse Cave*: Muir, *A Thousand-Mile Walk to the Gulf*, 10.

213 *"the most sublime and comprehensive picture"*: Muir, *A Thousand-Mile Walk to the Gulf*, 16.

214 *"knotted vines as remarkable for their efficient army"*: Muir, *A Thousand-Mile Walk to the Gulf*, 118.

215 *Muir then reached into his pocket*: Muir, *A Thousand-Mile Walk to the Gulf*, 104.

216 *for five nights in Bonaventure Cemetery*: Muir, *A Thousand-Mile Walk to the Gulf*, 77.

217 *put his journey on hold*: Muir, *A Thousand-Mile Walk to the Gulf*, 129.

218 *"This had very good success"*: Linklater, *Owning the Earth*, 25.

219 *Winthrop said that land is free*: Linklater, *Owning the Earth*, 27.

220 *To Benjamin Franklin*: Benjamin Franklin, "Queries and Remarks respecting Alterations in the Constitution of Pennsylvania," 1789, http://press-pubs.uchicago.edu.

221 *Thomas Paine in* Agrarian Justice: Thomas Paine, *Agrarian Justice*, 1797, https://www.ssa.gov.

222 *John Adams thought*: Freyfogle, *The Land We Share*, 53.

223 *A bill James Madison introduced*: Freyfogle, *The Land We Share*, 54.

224 *The Revolution, according to historian Gregory Alexander*: Freyfogle, *The Land We Share*, 80.

225 *"The central dilemma of American politics"*: Freyfogle, *The Land We Share*, 56.

226 *George Washington, after the Revolutionary War*: George Washington, "Washington's Circular Letter of Farewell to the Army," June 8, 1783, Library of Congress, http://www.loc.gov.

227 *Things were no different decades later in Jacksonian America*: Freyfogle, *The Land We Share*, 78–79.

228 *Virginia imposed a twice-yearly tax*: Freyfogle, *The Land We Share*, 54.

229 *Biographer Page Smith*: Page Smith, *John Adams* (Westport: Greenwood Press, 1969), 9–10.

230 *As a boy, Jefferson*: Claude Gernade Bowers, *The Young Jefferson* (Boston: Houghton Mifflin, 1969), 13.

231 *George Washington's boyhood residence*: Ron Chernow, *Washington: A Life* (New York: Penguin, 2010), 8.

232 *In 1748, a sixteen-year-old Washington*: Chernow, *Washington*, 19.

233 *As a boy, Benjamin Franklin*: Benjamin Franklin, *Autobiography of Benjamin Franklin* (New York: Henry Holt and Company, 1916), https://www.gutenberg.org. Walter Isaacson, *Benjamin Franklin: An American Life* (New York: Simon & Schuster, 2004), 16.

234 *the experiment probably took place*: Philip Dray, *Stealing God's Thunder* (New York: Random House, 2005), 85.

235 *As a boy, Ulysses roamed*: Ronald C. White Jr., *American Ulysses: A Life of Ulysses S. Grant* (New York: Random House, 2016), 15.

236 *In 1850, less than 10 percent of the South was enclosed*: Freyfogle, *On Private Property*, 30–31.

237 *"America was the land of liberty"*: Freyfogle, *On Private Property*, xv–xvi.

238 *1818 case in South Carolina*: Freyfogle, *On Private Property*, 38–39.

239 *Four years later, the court ruled*: Freyfogle, *On Private Property*, 42–43.

240 *The public felt at such liberty*: Freyfogle, *On Private Property*, 41.

241 *Virginia allowed people to mine for ores*: Freyfogle, *The Land We Share*, 58.

242 *Juries were friendly to so-called trespassers*: Freyfogle, *On Private Property*, 41–42.

243 *Orrando P. Dexter bought*: Freyfogle, *On Private Property*, 43–44.

244 *When owners tried to control*: Freyfogle, *On Private Property*, 46–47.

245 *For weeks Twain and his friends*: Ron Powers, *Dangerous Waters: A Biography of the Boy Who Became Mark Twain* (New York: Basic Books, 1999), 83.

246 *Twain fished*: Powers, *Dangerous Waters*, 100–101.

247 *Louisa May Alcott*: Susan Cheever, *Louisa May Alcott: A Personal Biography* (New York: Simon & Schuster, 2011), 3.

248 *"Something born of the lovely hour"*: Cheever, *Louisa May Alcott*, 39.

249 *Nebraska author Willa Cather*: Sharon O'Brien, *Willa Cather: The Emerging Voice* (Oxford: Oxford University Press, 1986), 68.

250 *Whitman wrote that he spent*: Walt Whitman, *Specimen Days* (Philadelphia: David McKay, 1892). From chapter "Paumanok, and My Life on It as Child and Young Man."

251 *Ernest Hemingway*: Jeffrey Meyers, *Hemingway: A Biography* (Boston: Da Capo, 1999), 13–15.

252 *"When I slide under a barbed-wire fence"*: Annie Dillard, *Pilgrim at Tinker Creek* (New York: HarperCollins, 1999), 6–7.

253 *Leonard Black, a slave*: Leonard Black, *The Life and Sufferings of Leonard Black* (New Bedford: Benjamin Lindsey, 1847), 26–27, http://docsouth.unc.edu.

254 *in thickets, cornfields, and creek bottoms*: Fergus M. Bordewich, *Bound for Canaan: The Epic Story of the Underground Railroad* (New York: HarperCollins, 2005), 232.

255 *"Thanks to her years in lumber camps"*: Bordewich, *Bound for Canaan*, 352.

256 *They hunted, fished, gardened*: David Blight, ed., *Passages to Freedom: The Underground Railroad in History and Memory* (Washington DC: Smithsonian, 2001).

257 *"thousands of Swallows were flying"*: Richard Rhodes, *John James Audubon: The Making of an American* (New York: Vintage, 2004), 58.

258 *Roosevelt was a sickly and asthmatic youth*: Douglas Brinkley, *The Wilderness Warrior: Theodore Roosevelt and the Crusade for America* (New York: HarperCollins, 2009), 93.

259 *The young Leopold*: Curt Meine, *Aldo Leopold: His Life and Work* (Madison: University of Wisconsin Press, 1988), 26.

260 *Leopold was off on daily tramps*: Meine, *Aldo Leopold*, 35–36.

261 *near her home in Pennsylvania*: Linda Lear, *Rachel Carson: Witness for Nature* (New York: Henry Holt & Co., 1997), 34 and 54.

262 *"looking in the tide pools"*: Lear, *Rachel Carson*, 61.

263 *"I think that I cannot preserve my health and spirits"*: Thoreau, "Walking."

264 *After the Civil War*: Freyfogle, *On Private Property*, 44–45.

265 *When the Louisiana legislature met*: Brian Sawers, "Property Law as Labor Control in the Postbellum South," *Law and History Review* 33 (2015): 361.

266 *An 1873 ruling by the New York Supreme Court*: Freyfogle, *The Land We Share*, 74.

267 *"Many courts became hostile"*: Freyfogle, *On Private Property*, 70.

268 *"Oh Mother Earth!"*: Arthur B. Baker, "No Trespassing," *Arizona Sentinel and Yuma Weekly Examiner*, March 25, 1915. Chronicling America, Library of Congress, http://chroniclingamerica.loc.gov.

269 *In England, requests such as these*: Jerry Anderson, "Countryside Access and Environmental Protection: An American View of Britain's Right to Roam," *Environmental Law Review* 9 (2007): 250.

270 *"one of the most essential sticks"*: Anderson, "Britain's Right to Roam," 426–27.

271 *says property law scholar Brian Sawers*: Sawers, "The Right to Exclude from Unimproved Land," 666–67.

272 *The case dealt with a cable company*: Anderson, "Countryside Access and Environmental Protection," 250–51.

273 *a walker is less of a nuisance than a train*: Anderson, "Countryside Access and Environmental Protection," 252.

274 *The Surfrider Foundation*: Pete Stauffer, "Let's Do This! Surfrider's Priorities for 2017," January 3, 2017, Surfrider Foundation, https://www.surfrider.org.

275 *In his encyclical,* Laudato Si': Pope Francis. *Laudato Si'*, 2015.

276 *According to the Safe Routes to School organization*: "Quick Facts and Stats," Safe Routes to School, http://www.saferoutespartnership.org.

277 *According to a General Social Survey*: "Public Trust Has Dwindled with Rise in Income Inequality," Association for Psychological Science, September 4, 2014.

278 *Rates of rape, robbery, aggravated assault*: Accessed online: http://www.bjs.gov/ and https://www.fbi.gov/.

279 *We are two times less likely*: "State-by-state and national crime estimates by year," Bureau of Justice Statistics, http://www.bjs.gov/.

280 *"There's a five-letter word"*: Elinor Ostrom. "Notes on complexity, communication and trust: IU's Ostrom delivers Nobel lecture to worldwide audience," Indiana University, December 8, 2009.

281 *Katherine Hawley sums up Ostrom's*: Katherine Hawley, *Trust: A Very Short Introduction* (Oxford: Oxford University Press, 2012), 27.

282 *Our schools are more segregated by race*: Emily Richmond, "Schools are more segregated today than during the late 1960s," *The Atlantic,* June 11, 2012.

283 *we are segregated by age*: Leon Neyfakh, "What 'age segregation' does to America," *Boston Globe*, August 31, 2014.

284 *There is income segregation*: Richard Fry and Paul Taylor, "The Rise of Residential Segregation by Income," Pew Research Center, August 1, 2012.

285 *The authors of* Suburban Nation: Andrés Duany, Elizabeth Plater-Zyberk, Jeff Speck, *Suburban Nation: The Rise of Sprawl and the Decline of the American Dream* (New York: North Point, 2000), 46.

286 *data from a Pew Research Center survey*: Niraj Chokshi, "US partisanship is highest in decades, Pew study finds," *New York Times,* June 23, 2016.

287 *As* The New York Times *sums up these studies*: Elizabeth Dunn and Michael Norton, "Hello, stranger," *New York Times,* April 25, 2014.

288 *According to a Swedish study*: Richard Louv, *Last Child in the Woods: Saving Our Children from Nature-Deficit Disorder* (Chapel Hill: Algonquin, 2008), 51.

289 *According to the Organisation for Economic Co-operation and Development's*: "How's Life, 2015," OECD, 2015, 126.

290 *according to Richard Louv*: Louv, *Last Child in the Woods*, 18–19.

291 *Eighty-one percent of us live in urban*: "World Urbanization Prospects: The 2014 Revision," United Nations, 2015, 50.

292 *60 percent of us live in large metropolises*: Dan Rubinstein, *Born to Walk: The Transformative Power of a Pedestrian Act* (Toronto: ECW Press, 2015), 24.

293 *Rhonda L. Clements*: Louv, *Last Child in the Woods*, 34–35.

294 *The more we live our lives indoors*: Rubinstein, *Born to Walk*, 18–19.

295 *Hippocrates, the Greek physician*: Rubinstein, *Born to Walk*, 18.

296 *The analysis found that moderate walking*: Rubinstein, *Born to Walk*, 18–19.

297 *Stanford graduate student Gregory Bratmana*: Gregory N. Bratmana, Gretchen C. Daily, Benjamin J. Levy, James J. Gross, "The benefits of nature experience: Improved affect and cognition," *Landscape and Urban Planning* 138 (2015): 41.

298 *Richard Louv in* Vitamin N: Richard Louv, *Vitamin N: The Essential Guide to a Nature-Rich Life* (Chapel Hill: Algonquin, 2016), 59.

299 *Forests, Li said*: Rubinstein, *Born to Walk*, 26.

300 *A Scottish Natural Heritage study*: Ruth Jepson, Roma Robertson, Heather Cameron, "Green prescription schemes: mapping and current practice," Scottish Natural Heritage (2010): 8.

301 *In the United Kingdom, physical inactivity*: "Making
     the case for physical activity," BHF National
     Centre, 1.

302 *The American Diabetes Association*: "The Cost of
     Diabetes," American Diabetes Association, last
     modified June 22, 2015.

303 *In 2012, the Integrated Benefits Institute*: Sarah
     Kliff, "Poor health costs employers $576
     billion," *Washington Post*, September 14,
     2012.

304 *According to the Centers for Disease Control and
     Prevention*: Susan A. Carlson, Janet E. Fulton,
     Michael Pratt, Zhou Yang, E. Kathleen Adams,
     "Inadequate Physical Activity and Health Care
     Expenditures in the United States," *Progress in
     Cardiovascular Diseases* 57 (2015): 317.

305 *Hundreds of thousands of dollars were spent*: W.
     Hodding Carter, "The Near-Impossible Process of
     Making a National Park," *Outside*, July 19, 2016.

306 *"What in blazes"*: Juliet Eilperin and Brady Dennis,
     "Obama creates what could be the last large
     national park site on the East Coast, in Maine,"
     Washington Post, August 24, 2016.

307 *The public lands in Sweden*: "Protected Nature,"
     Statistics Sweden.

308 *$3 billion annual budget*: Nathan Rott, "National
     parks have a long to-do list but can't cover the repair
     costs," NPR, March 8, 2016.

309 *331 million visits*: Katia Hetter, "America's most
     popular national parks are . . ." CNN, March 10,
     2017.

310 *Yosemite National Park warns*: "Traffic in Yosemite
     National Park," Yosemite National Park, https://
     www.nps.gov/yose.

311 *Great Smoky Mountains National Park*: Hetter,
     "America's most popular national parks are . . ."

312 *Outdoor recreation is also growing*: "Outdoor Recreation Participation Topline Report, 2016," Outdoor Foundation, 1,5, & 8.

313 *an unprecedented reservation system*: John Hollenhorst, "Jammed highway lights fire under Arches controversy," *Deseret News*, May 31, 2015.

314 *"We're running out of room"*: Kirk Siegler, "Long lines, packed campsites and busy trails: Our crowded national parks," NPR, March 7, 2016.

315 *The landowner still has the right*: Campion and Stephenson, "The 'right to roam,'" 22.

316 *There are more than four hundred*: Campion and Stephenson, "The 'right to roam,'" 23.

317 *four thousand nature reserves*: "Swedes love nature," official website of Sweden, https://sweden.se.

318 *the Prairie Plains Resource Institute*: Lauren Sedam, "Prairie Plains Resource Institute almost ready to buy Sherman Ranch," *Grand Island Independent*, July 10, 2015.

319 *The Prairie Reserve's goal*: "Building the Reserve," American Prairie Reserve, https://www.american prairie.org.

320 *were officially secured in 2014*: "Our History," Appalachian Trail Conservancy, http://www .appalachiantrail.org.

321 *obtaining 3,700 small tracts*: Brian King and Javier Folger, "Land Acquisition Leader Retiring from Appalachian Trail Conservancy," Appalachian Trail Conservancy, April 19, 2011, http://www.appala chiantrail.org.

322 *$24 a night for a campsite*: Camping costs were gathered from the various parks' websites in winter 2017.

323 *Leitch imagined a park service*: William C. Leitch, "Backpacking in 2078," *Sierra Club Bulletin* 63 (1978): 25–27.

324 *Jack Turner, in* The Abstract Wild: Jack Turner, *The Abstract Wild* (Tucson: University of Arizona, 1996), 16.

325 *Between 1990 and 2013*: "Federal Land Ownership," 15.

326 *cropland and forests will decline*: Paul Bolstad, Samuel D. Brody, David Hulse, Roger Kroh, Thomas R. Loveland, Allison Thomson, "Land Use and Land Cover Change," US Global Change Research Program, http://nca2014.globalchange.gov.

327 *3.7 percent of the US population*: Population data taken from 2010 US Census, http://www.census.gov.

328 *according to the Land Trust Alliance's*: "National Land Trust Census Report," Land Trust Alliance, 2015, 5 & 8.

329 *to purchase easements*: "Public Access to BLM Managed Public Lands: A Report to the House Appropriations Committee," 3.

330 *Of the 566 Fish and Wildlife refuges*: From an email interview with Vanessa Kauffman, a spokeswoman at the US Fish and Wildlife Service (February 27, 2017): "Of the nation's 566 national wildlife refuges, 462 are open to public use and recreation. Most of the remaining 104 refuges are closed for resource protection, but some may be closed for public safety reasons, staffing shortages or other reasons. Within those refuges that are open-to-the-public, some portions may be closed either year-round or seasonally due to resource protection."

331 *Of these 197 million acres*: I got the 18 million number from "Statistical Report of State Park Operations: 2013–2014," National Association of State Park Directors, 9. The table on page nine in the report compiled acreage from states that adds up state parks, recreation areas, natural areas, historic areas, among others. I got the 197 million number from "Public Land Ownership by State," National Wilderness Institute, 1995, http://www.nrcm.org.

332 *US Census Bureau shows*: Colby, "Projections of the Size and Composition of the US Population: 2014 to 2060," 1.

333 *expulsion of the land's inhabitants*: Karl Jacoby, *Crimes Against Nature: Squatters, Poachers, Thieves, and the Hidden History of American Conservation* (Berkeley: University of California Press, 2014), 151.

334 *soldiers pushed out the Ahwahneechee*: Julian Brave, "The Forgotten History of 'Violent Displacement' That Helped Create the National Parks," *Huffington Post*, August 26, 2015.

335 *How we protect nature*: William Cronon, "In Search of Nature," an essay in *Uncommon Ground: Rethinking the Human Place in Nature* (New York: W. W. Norton & Co., 1995), 69–90.

336 *Surveys from Pew Research*: Carl Brown, "See America First: Public Opinion and National Parks," Roper Center, Cornell University, May 9, 2016.

337 *Visibility has dropped 80 percent*: This air quality paragraph comes from two sources: "Air Quality," Great Smoky Mountains National Park, https://www.nps.gov/grsm/; Donald W. Linzey, *A Natural History Guide to Great Smoky Mountains National Park* (Knoxville: The University of Tennessee Press, 2008), 208.

338 *the 1,336 Superfund*: "Superfund: National Priorities List," Environmental Protection Agency, last modified June 16, 2017.

339 *In his widely cited essay*: William Cronon, "The Trouble with Wilderness; or, Getting Back to the Wrong Nature," an essay in *Uncommon Ground: Rethinking the Human Place in Nature* (New York: W. W. Norton & Co., 1995), 69–90, http://www.williamcronon.net. All subsequent Cronon quotes come from this essay.

340 *Author Michael Lewis*: Michael Lewis, "Wilderness and Conservation Science," in *American Wilderness:*

A New History, ed. Michael Lewis (New York: Oxford University Press, 2007), 9.

341 *Where the top half of 1 percent*: Charles Geisler, "Land and Poverty," *Land Economics* 71 (1995): 19.

342 *Between 1887 and 1934*: Gilbert, "Who Owns the Land?" 57.

343 *confined to tiny lots*: Monte Burke, "John Malone Overtakes Ted Turner as Largest Individual Landowner in the US," *Forbes,* March 10, 2011.

344 *Where minority groups*: Isabelle Anguelovski, "From Toxic Sites to Parks as (Green) LULUs?" *Journal of Planning Literature* 31 (2016): 25.

345 *Our likelihood of achieving economic success*: Stephen J. Dubner, "Is the American Dream Really Dead?" *Freakonomics,* January 18, 2017, http://freakonomics .com; Raj Chetty, "The Fading American Dream," National Bureau of Economic Research, December 2016, 18, figures 4, s3, & 8, http://www.equality-of -opportunity.org/; David Leonhardt, "In climbing income ladder, location matters," *New York Times,* July 22, 2013.

346 *Author Gregory Clark*: Evan Horowitz, "You have better luck with the American dream in Denmark," *Boston Globe,* October 17, 2016.

347 *767,000 Swedes*: Interview with Anna Grundén, July 2016: "In 2016 around 767,000 people participated in the Keep Sweden Tidy cleanup campaign. 274 municipalities participated in the campaign. Approximately 135,000 are adults of the total amount of participants."

348 *adults regularly smoked*: "Achievements in Public Health, 1900-1999: Tobacco Use—United States, 1900-1999," CDC, 1999, https://www.cdc.gov.

349 *By 2015, only 15 percent*: "Current Cigarette Smoking Among Adults in the United States," CDC, https://www.cdc.gov.

350 *Or consider seat belt use*: "How States Achieve High
     Seat Belt Use Rates," National Highway Traffic
     Safety Administration, August 2008, pages 1, 4, and
     i, https://crashstats.nhtsa.dot.gov/.

351 *seat belt use in 2014*: "Seat Belt Use in 2014—Use
     Rates in the States and Territories," National
     Highway Traffic Safety Administration, June 2015,
     https://crashstats.nhtsa.dot.gov.

352 *"Crying Indian" commercial*: William O'Barr, "Public
     Service Advertising and Propaganda," *Advertising &
     Society Review*, 13 (2012).

353 *They got Texas celebrities*: "Reducing Litter on
     Roadsides," National Cooperative Highway
     Research Program, Transportation Research Board
     (2009): 33–35.

354 *The first is an "invitee"*: Michael J. Lunn, "Class
     Dismissed: Forty-nine Years Later, Recreational
     Statutes Finally Align with Legislation's Original
     Intent," *Drake Journal of Agricultural Law* 20 (2015):
     139–143.

355 *English landowners can sleep easy*: "Open access land:
     management, rights and responsibilities," UK
     Government, September 17, 2014.

356 *a risk resulting*: Countryside and Rights of Way Act
     2000, 13 (2) (6A), http://www.legislation.gov.uk.

357 *there were 11,961 homicides*: "2014 Crime in the
     United States," FBI, https://ucr.fbi.gov.

358 *mostly contained to cities*: "Homicide Trends in the
     United States, 1980–2008," Bureau of Justice
     Statistics, November 2011, 30.

359 *acquaintances and family members commit*: "Homicide
     Trends in the United States, 1980–2008," 16,
     table 8.

360 *A stranger killing a stranger*: "Homicide Trends in the
     United States, 1980–2008," 16.

361   *"Trespassers will be shot"*: Cindy Horswell, "Boy's death could upgrade Liberty couple's charges," *Houston Chronicle*, May 8, 2009.

362   *two men in West Virginia were shot*: "Details of deadly Cabell shootings surface in court documents," WSAZ News Channel, January 27, 2014.

363   *a Japanese exchange student*: "Defense depicts Japanese boy as 'scary,'" *New York Times*, May 21, 1993.

364   *The International Hunter Education Association*: International Hunter Education Association, http://www.ihea-usa.org.

365   *14 million of whom go hunting*: "2011 National Survey of Fishing, Hunting, and Wildlife-Associated Recreation," US Fish and Wildlife Service, 28. Revised February 2014, http://www.census.gov.

366   *Of the top ten industrialized Western countries*: "Estimated number of guns per capita by country," Wikipedia. Accessed July 12, 2017. The Wikipedia entry borrows mostly from *Small Arms Survey 2007: Guns and the City* (Cambridge: Cambridge University Press, 2007).

367   *This is similar to the ratio in Scandinavian countries*: "Hunters in Europe," FACE: The European Federation of Associations for Hunting & Conservation, http://www.face.eu.

368   *Americans legally allowed to kill trespassers*: Section 9.31 of Texas penal code, http://www.statutes.legis.state.tx.us.

369   *Consider the case of Markus Hendrick Kaarma*: James Queally, "Montana man who trapped, killed German student gets 70-year sentence," *Los Angeles Times*, February 12, 2015.

370   *Kaarma could not prove that*: "Montana Code Annotated 2015," 45-3-103: Use of force in defense of occupied structure, http://leg.mt.gov.

371   *Rodney Bruce Black*: Kaitlynn LeBeau, "Cabell County man ruled incompetent in double murder," WSAZ3, January 8, 2016.

372 *Sheila Muhs*: Bob Horn Jr., "Muhs given life term for murder," *Star Courier*.

373 *Japanese exchange student*: Adam Nossiter, "Judge awards damages in Japanese youth's death," *New York Times*, September 16, 1994.

374 *who live in apartments*: "Quick Facts: Resident Demographics," National Multifamily Housing Council, http://www.nmhc.org/. Source for their tables is "2015 American Community Survey, 1-Year Estimates," US Census Bureau. Updated September 2016.

375 *According to the Census Bureau*: "US Cities Are Home to 62.7 Percent of the US Population, but Comprise Just 3.5 Percent of Land Area," US Census Bureau, March 4, 2015, http://www.census.gov.

376 *The top five "shortchanged" states*: Steven Johnson, "Why blue states are the real 'Tea Party,'" *New York Times*, December 3, 2016.

377 *A 2012 Pew Research center survey*: Rich Morin, Paul Taylor, Eileen Patten, "A Bipartisan Nation of Beneficiaries," Pew Research Center, December 18, 2012.

378 *taxpayers give $20 billion*: "Farm Programs," US Government Accountability Office, http://www.gao.gov.

379 *taxpayer money on fire suppression*: "Federal Firefighting Costs (Suppression Only) 1985–2016," National Interagency Fire Center, https://www.nifc.gov.

380 *Atlanta metro area paid*: Aaron M. Renn, "Reforming anti-urban bias in transportation spending," *New Geography*, February 4, 2010.

381 *In 1950, 64 percent of Americans*: "World Urbanization Prospects: The 2014 Revision," 212.

382 *In 2014, it was 81 percent*: "World Urbanization Prospects: The 2014 Revision," 50.

383 *steady decline in our rural population*: "World Urbanization Prospects: The 2014 Revision," 237.

384 *huge increase in our urban population*: "World Urbanization Prospects: The 2014 Revision," 225.

385 *87 percent urban*: "World Urbanization Prospects: The 2014 Revision," 225 and 249.

386 *recognizing zoning ordinances*: "When and why was zoning created?" NYC Department of City Planning, https://www1.nyc.gov/.

387 *Maine's legislature enacted*: "Public Shoreline Access in Maine: A Citizen's Guide to Ocean and Coastal Law," University of Maine Sea Grant College Program and the University of Maine School of Law, August 2016, third edition, 5–6.

388 *Vermont's 1777 state constitution*: Sawers, "The Right to Exclude from Unimproved Land," 678.

389 *in Vermont you have a right*: Vermont Constitution, established July 9, 1793, and amended through December 14, 2010, #67, http://legislature.vermont .gov.

390 *In a New Jersey Supreme Court case*: Sawers, "The Right to Exclude from Unimproved Land," 672.

391 *In Maine, Massachusetts, and Virginia*: Tannenbaum, "Surfrider Foundation's Stance on Beach Access."

392 *Scottish Code*: Scottish Outdoor Access Code, Scottish Natural Heritage, 2005, 5–6, http://www .snh.org.uk.

393 *But advances in women's rights*: Harvey Jacobs, "Private property and human rights: A mismatch in the 21st century?" *International Journal of Social Welfare* 22 (2013): 98.

394 *Trails and bike paths*: Megan Lawson, "Measuring Trails Benefits: Property Value," *Headwaters Economics*, spring 2016, http://headwaterseconomics.org.

395 *One rails-to-trail conversion*: Josh Barbanel, "The High Line's 'halo effect' on property," *Wall Street Journal*, August 7, 2016.

396 *The inhabitants of the several states*: "The Address and reasons of dissent of the minority of the convention, of the state of Pennsylvania, to their constituents (excerpt)," Library of Congress, December 12, 1787, Amendment 8, https://www.archives.gov.

397 *"harpies of power"*: "The Address and reasons of dissent of the minority of the convention, of the state of Pennsylvania, to their constituents (excerpt)," Library of Congress, December 12, 1787, https://www.archives.gov.

398 *Conservation is a pipe-dream*: Eric Freyfogle, *A Good That Transcends: How US Culture Undermines Environmental Reform* (Chicago: University of Chicago, 2017), 16.

399 *Locke's theory articulated*: I don't wish to besmirch Locke's reputation here, as his theory on property was, in ways, both forward thinking and just. Locke has been embraced by libertarians for his belief in the right for individuals to own land and the matter-of-fact way in which land can be obtained. Yet we must remember that Locke said that we can only acquire land if we use it productively (and don't simply own it as giant and unproductive estates), which means that each person's portion of land will actually be, in Locke's vision, quite small, especially since, in 1689 when Locke wrote his *Two Treatises*, one man could only do so much work, without the help of a tractor and an army of migrant fieldworkers. Because someone could not "consume more than a small part" of land, Locke wrote, it is "impossible for any man . . . to entrench upon the right of another." Furthermore, Locke believed that one could claim land only if there was enough land around for other folks to claim their own. Andro Linklater in *Owning*

the Earth calls Locke "revolutionary," not for Locke's crafty labor-mixing philosophies but for Locke's devotion to justice and fairness.

400 *According to Aldo Leopold*: Freyfogle, *The Land We Share*, 281.

401 *"The average citizen"*: Freyfogle, *The Land We Share*, 150.

402 *Leopold wanted to expand*: Aldo Leopold, *A Sand County Almanac* (Oxford: Oxford University Press, 1987), 204.

403 *"The land of every country"*: John Stuart Mill, *Principles of Political Economy with Some of Their Applications to Social Philosophy,* Book II, Chapter II.

404 *In February of 1940*: Robert Santelli, *This Land Is Your Land: Woody Guthrie and the Journey of an American Folk Song* (Philadelphia: Running Press, 2012), 7.

405 *in response to Irving Berlin's*: Niraj Chokshi, "Who owns the copyright to 'This Land Is Your Land'? It may be you and me," *New York Times*, June 17, 2016.

Index